Keto]
Beginners

Essential Guide to Ketogenic Diet for Weight Loss, Body Healing and Living a Keto Lifestyle.

57 Delectable Low-Carbohydrate Easy Recipes and a 21-Day Meal Plan

Dr. James Berry

Text Copyright © Dr. James Berry

All rights reserved. No part of this guide may be reproduced in any form without permission in writing from the publisher except in the case of brief quotations embodied in critical articles or reviews.

Legal & Disclaimer

The information contained in this book and its contents is not designed to replace or take the place of any form of medical or professional advice; and is not meant to replace the need for independent medical, financial, legal or other professional advice or services, as may be required. The content and information in this book has been provided for educational and entertainment purposes only.

The content and information contained in this book has been compiled from sources deemed reliable, and it is accurate to the best of the Author's knowledge, information, and belief. However, the Author cannot guarantee its accuracy and validity and cannot be held liable for any errors and/or omissions. Further, changes are periodically made to this book as and when needed. Where appropriate and/or necessary, you must consult a professional (including but not limited to your doctor, attorney, financial advisor or such other professional advisor) before using any of the suggested remedies, techniques, or information in this book.

Upon using the contents and information contained in this book, you agree to hold harmless the Author from and against any damages, costs, and expenses, including any legal fees potentially resulting from the application of any of the information provided by this book. This disclaimer applies to any loss, damages or injury caused by the use and application, whether directly or indirectly, of any advice or information presented, whether for breach of contract, tort, negligence, personal injury, criminal intent, or under any other cause of action.

You agree to accept all risks of using the information presented inside this book.

You agree that by continuing to read this book, where appropriate and/or necessary, you shall consult a professional (including but not limited to your doctor, attorney, or financial advisor or such other advisor as needed) before using any of the suggested remedies, techniques, or information in this book

Table of Contents

Introduction

Congratulations on purchasing <u>Keto Diet for Beginners</u>, and thank you for it! You have taken an important step by deciding to follow this diet. This book will provide you with the necessary tools to quickly start using the Keto Diet to improve your appearance, health, and well-being.

We know that the keto diet for newbies looks exciting, but at the same time, it can be a daunting and confusing process at first.

To help you figure this out, we will share tricks in the following chapters, and talk about important points and features of the keto diet. Starting with a detailed description of what a ketogenic diet is and what kinds there are, we will demonstrate in detail the many benefits of a Keto Diet, while revealing the basic rules. You will receive tips and advice to help you solve any problems with the keto diet, as well as tips for success.

The book contains delicious easy recipes and a 3-week nutrition plan, thanks to which you can easily begin your journey to keto.

Thank you again for choosing this particular book. We created this book to be as informative and understandable as possible, so that readers would be comfortable exploring the world of keto, so please enjoy!

Chapter 1 – What Is the Ketogenic Diet?

The keto diet is well known as a low-carb diet, during which the body produces ketones in the liver and uses them as energy. It is called by many different names: a ketogenic or ketone diet, a low carbohydrate diet, a low sugar diet (LCHF), etc.

When you eat something rich in carbohydrates, your body will produce glucose and insulin.

Glucose is the simplest molecule in your body that is converted and used as energy, so that it will take precedence over any other source of energy.

Insulin is produced to process blood glucose.

Since glucose is used as primary energy, fats are not involved in any way and therefore accumulate.

Usually, on a normal diet with a higher carbohydrate content, the body will use glucose as the main form of energy. By decreasing carbohydrate intake, the body enters a condition known as ketosis.

Ketosis is a natural process that helps our body survive during hunger. During this condition, we produce ketones, which are formed during the breakdown of fats in the liver.

The ultimate goal of a properly maintained ketone diet is to get your body into this metabolic state. But we will do this not by reducing calories, but by reducing carbohydrates.

Our bodies are incredibly adapted to what you invest in - when you overload it with fats and select carbohydrates, it will begin to burn ketones as the primary source of energy. Optimal ketone levels provide many benefits in terms of health, weight loss, mental and physical characteristics.

With this diet, you will not feel hungry, and at the same time, you will increase your activity and improve your health. Yes, But that's not all that the ketogenic diet is suitable for. This is just the top tip of the keto iceberg!

Why is Keto Diet Safe?

Firstly, it is the most natural way of eating for a person. Tens of thousands of years ago, our ancestors ate mainly things that were hunted. They were athletic, quick, and energetic. Our genetics and the structure of humans have not changed much since then. But what has changed?

A few thousand years ago, agriculture appeared; carbohydrates were added to the diet, and the consumption of a massive amount of sugar (which is happening in modern times), was started around 50-60 years ago. Why did they live on average more than us? It is mainly associated with medicine and hygiene.

Second, the keto diet comes from medicine, where it is used to control the symptoms of epilepsy, cancer, diabetes, and other diseases.

Thirdly, there is not a single study that has revealed harm from the correct keto diet. All problems from increased fat intake are associated with the consumption of abnormal fats and increased use of carbohydrates.

10 Proven Benefits of Keto Diet

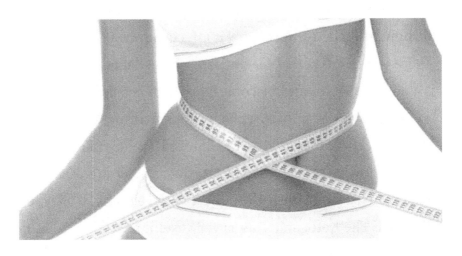

Low carb diets can reduce your appetite. Any diet increases hunger, and this is usually the main problem of dieting. It is the main reason why many people feel unhappy and eventually give up. Perhaps it is an accident that the word diet (nutrition) begins with the word (die) - to die. However, the use of low-carb foods leads to an automatic decrease in appetite. By reducing carbohydrate intake and increasing fat and protein intake, the total amount of calories eaten drops.

Low-carb diets lead to high weight loss. Reducing carbohydrate intake is one of the easiest and most effective ways to lose weight. Studies show that people on a low carbohydrate diet lose weight faster than people on a lean diet, even with substantial calorie restriction.

First of all, fat from the abdomen (abdominal fat) goes. Fat can be stored in different places. The location of fat accumulation determines how it affects our health.

There are two types of fat deposits: subcutaneous fat, which is under the skin, and visceral fat, which accumulates in the abdominal cavity and is typically found in most overweight men. Visceral fat envelops the internal organs and impairs their performance. Excess visceral fat is typically associated with increased inflammation and the development of type 2 diabetes. The Ketogenic Diet is very useful in getting rid of fat on the abdomen.

Significantly lowers triglycerides. Triglycerides are fat molecules that circulate in the blood. It is well known that fasting triglycerides are one of the signs of an increased risk of heart disease. The main reason for the high level of triglycerides in people living a sedentary lifestyle is the consumption of large amounts of carbohydrates, mainly pure sucrose and fructose. When people reduce carbohydrate intake, there is a very sharp decrease in the level of triglycerides in the blood. Also, keep in mind that low-fat diets often lead to an increase in triglyceride levels.

Increasing the level of "good" HDL cholesterol

High-density lipoprotein (HDL) is often called "good" cholesterol. The higher your HDL level compared to "bad" LDL, the lower the risk of heart disease. One of the best ways to increase "good" cholesterol is to eat healthy fat, and low-carb diets contain a lot of fat. It is therefore not surprising that HDL levels increase dramatically on healthy diets low in carbohydrates (for example, keto diets), while, on regular diets, the level of "good" cholesterol rises slightly.

Decreased blood sugar and insulin levels

Low-carb diets can also be especially helpful for people with diabetes and insulin resistance, which affects millions of people around the world. Studies show that reducing carbohydrates dramatically reduces blood sugar and insulin levels. Some people with diabetes who are starting a keto diet may need to immediately reduce their insulin dose by 50%. In one study on people with type 2 diabetes, 95% reduced or stopped taking glucose-lowering drugs for six months. If you are taking blood sugar medications, talk with your doctor before making changes to carbohydrate intake, as your dosage may need to be adjusted to prevent hypoglycemia.

Normalization of blood pressure

High blood pressure, or hypertension, is a significant risk factor for many diseases, including heart disease, stroke, and renal failure. Low-carb diets are an effective way to lower blood pressure, which should reduce the risk of these diseases and help you live longer. Please note - if you start a keto diet and at the same time take pills to normalize blood pressure, you should consult with your doctor to adjust the dose of the medicine.

Keto diet is effective against metabolic syndrome

Metabolic syndrome is a condition closely associated with the risk of developing diabetes and heart disease. In fact, metabolic syndrome is a combination of symptoms that include: Abdominal obesity, High blood pressure, high fasting blood sugar, High triglycerides, Low "good" HDL cholesterol, Low-carb diets, especially keto diets, are incredibly effective in treating all five of these symptoms.

Keto diet leads to a reduction in LDL "bad" cholesterol

People who have high "bad" LDL (low-density lipoprotein) have an increased risk of worsening cardiovascular diseases due to vascular problems. However, particle size is important. Smaller particles are associated with a higher risk of cardiovascular disease, while larger particles are associated with a lower risk. Thus, reducing carbohydrate intake can significantly reduce the likelihood of heart and vessel problems.

The ketogenic (keto) diet is used in medicine to treat certain diseases of the brain

Your brain needs glucose, as some of its parts can only receive energy from it. That is why your liver produces glucose from protein if there is not enough carbohydrate (gluconeogenesis). However, most of your brain can also use ketones to generate energy. They are formed during fasting or significant restriction of carbohydrate intake. When the brain begins to receive energy from ketones, it greatly improves its condition and very beneficial effect on many processes. In one study, more than half of children on Ketogenic Diets experienced a reduction in the number of seizures by more than 50%, while 16% completely eliminated all symptoms. Very low-carb diets are currently being studied for the treatment of other brain diseases, such as Alzheimer's and Parkinson's. In the popular health food literature, very little is said about the benefits of low-carb diets, such as Keto Diets. These diets not only improve your cholesterol, blood pressure and blood sugar, but also reduce your appetite, help you lose weight, and lower triglyceride levels. If you are interested in improving your health, you should think about one of the options for such a diet.

Who Should Avoid the Keto Diet?

- Type 1 diabetes
- gallbladder disease (or without a gallbladder)
- kidney disease
- liver disease
- pancreatic diseases
- increased pressure (pressure control and dose control of drugs) people with impaired metabolism
- people with a tendency to the formation of kidney stones (need attention to the change in the balance of fluid and salt)

Diet is not recommended for:
- Underweight people
- children under 18
- people after surgery
- pregnant or breastfeeding

Types of Keto Diets

1. Classical (medical) - it is calculated so that 75 percent of calories come from sources of fat, 5 percent from carbohydrates and 20 percent from protein. Usually, it is about 20 grams carbohydrates per day excluding fiber (insoluble carbohydrates).

2. Modern - not so strict version of the medical version of the diet, starting with 30 grams of carbohydrates per day. The calculation of the protein is based on the weight of a person, approximately 0.7-1.1 grams of protein per 1 kg of weight is taken.

3. Sports - similar to the previous version, but due to some difficulties in strength indicators, and with a minimum content of glycogen in the body during intensive sports activities, it is possible to add carbohydrates during strength exercises, along with going beyond the anaerobic threshold and increasing the level of protein intake.

4. Vegetarian Keto Diet or Vegan Keto Diet: Yes, both are possible. Instead of animal products, many vegetarian and/or low-carbohydrate foods are included. Nuts, seeds, low-carb fruits and vegetables, leafy greens, healthy fats, and dairy products - all of these are an excellent choice while on the vegetable keto-diet.

5. The "Dirty" Keto Diet is a distorted version of the diet due to the burst of interest in it and the emergence of a large number of "experts" on the Internet who, after reading a few articles, start an Instagram account and start teaching people how to follow the keto diet. At the same time, the correct distribution of CPFC (Calories Protein Fats Carbohydrates) is even claimed, but the attention is not paid to the balance of the diet, the saturation of vitamin and minerals, the quality of fats, etc. It allows you to eat anything, even bacon and heavily processed meats (with sugar and monosodium glutamate). There is also a diet option with the consumption of one meat food, while no attention is paid to the consumption of fiber and vegetables. Such options, of course, cannot be recommended for use. If you decide to follow this - do it at your own peril and risk; weigh all the risks and try to minimize such experiments in time.

6. "Lazy" Keto-Diet (Lazy Keto). This option is often confused with dirty keto, but they are very different, as "lazy" means simply not carefully tracking macros of fat and protein and calories. In principle, this is possible, but, but you need to strictly monitor the consumption of carbohydrates at the beginning not to exceed 30 grams of carbohydrates per day. Sometimes, this option may be easier for beginners, but you need to understand that the effects of such a diet will be much weaker.

7. Pure Keto is the most complete version of Keto Diet. In fact, it is a variant of the modern keto diet, but with an emphasis on balance and variety of diet. In modern Keto, it is allowed to take a large quantity of additives, minerals, and vitamins, because it is considered that it is very difficult to balance the Keto Diet. In the "clean" version of the diet this problem is solved, and all the necessary vitamins and minerals are taken from the diet as much as possible.

Chapter 2 - How to start a Keto Diet?

The basic rules of Keto Dieting

Next, consider some good rules about how to perform a keto diet regardless of its type.

1. Advice - go into Keto smoothly and slowly!

That is, it should not be that yesterday you ate a cake, and today you are already on Keto. We have to go gradually. Today, you choose one food group and pick them up, for example, rice or potatoes. On another day or in a week, you stop drinking beer and eating pizza, and then gradually remove the third group of products - it can be sweets (ice cream, shed, cakes, sweets, etc.)

2. Council-We trace Macros.

KETO DIET

75% FATS

20% CARBS

5% PROTEIN

Macronutrients are food substances (proteins, fats, and carbohydrates) necessary for an individual, and in quantities measured in grams. They provide energy, other needs of the body. Use the app that's convenient for you to track your macros.

> The ketosis formula looks like this: Proteins - 20% Fat - 75% Carbohydrates - 5%

If you strictly adhere to these proportions, then your body is in constant ketosis, that is, it takes energy not from glucose derived from carbohydrates, but from ketones synthesized from fat.

Fat.

The best part of the keto diet. They should be in the diet 60-75%. Fats, which we should prefer on the ketogenic diet, and surely take care of our health are divided into several categories: saturated fats, monounsaturated fats, polyunsaturated fats, and Trans fats of natural origin.

Saturated. The main benefits of the consumption of saturated fats for our body are: improving the ratio of high and low-density lipoprotein levels, maintaining bone density, stimulating the immune system, and supporting the production of the most essential hormones: cortisol and testosterone — sources of saturated fat: butter, fatty meat, cream, lard, coconut oil, eggs.

Monounsaturated fats have always been recognized as healthy and conducive to raising the level of good cholesterol and insulin sensitivity. Besides, these fats reduce blood pressure, help reduce the risk of cardiovascular diseases, and help reduce body fat.

The primary sources are: cold pressed olive oil, avocado and avocado oil, macadamia nut oil, goose fat, and bacon.

Polyunsaturated fats.

First, it is worth mentioning that the sources of these fats should be consumed, excluding heat because when heated, they form free radicals that increase inflammation and increase the risk of cancer and cardiovascular diseases.

The main benefits of these fats are in the content of omega 3 and omega 6 - essential elements in our diet. A healthy balance of these fatty acids helps reduce the risk of heart attacks and diseases of the immune system.

The primary sources are flax seeds and flaxseed oil, walnuts, oily fish and fish oil, sesame oil, chia seeds, and avocado oil.

Trans fats are of natural origin.

Do not be confused by the prefix "trans" in the name of this category. Here we will focus on Vaccenic acid, a trans-fat, found in foods such as animal meat, herbal supplements, and dairy sources of fat. The main benefits of vaccenic fatty acid consumption are a reduction in the risk of heart disease, diabetes, and obesity.

It is logical to move from this point to the so-called "bad" fats, the consumption of which we should keep to a minimum, or ideally, eliminate from our diets altogether.

Unhealthy processed Trans fats and polyunsaturated fats.

These fats acquire their negative characteristics during thermal processing. Here are the primary examples of fats, the use of which should be avoided: hydrogenated and partially hydrogenated oils used in the manufacturing of factory baked goods, crackers, and fast food, as well as vegetable oils such as cottonseed, sunflower, soybean, and canola oil

3. Advice- Watch for the amount of protein!

Protein.

Protein should be between 15 and 30% in your diet. The amount of protein should be limited because the body can convert protein into glucose through the process of gluconeogenesis. Excess glucose can also stop ketosis, erasing progress and wasting time.

Carbohydrates

You should always stay within the recommended range of pure carbohydrates. If you do not do this, you will not be able to get into or keep a state of ketosis, which will negate all your efforts for a healthy lifestyle.

If you consume too many carbohydrates, it is easy to feel:

• tired and sleepy after eating

• hungry quickly after eating

So, let's talk about the best carbohydrates during the keto diet.

4. Remove simple carbohydrates from the diet.

Always choose glucose, not fructose. Fructose replenishes glycogen stores in the liver, not in the muscles. Because of this, fructose will inhibit ketosis, while glucose will immediately go to work.

- You should eat healthy, complex carbohydrates, but at the same time watch your macros and the glycemic index of foods.

- Thus, the best carbohydrates include:

- Asparagus

- Artichokes

- Broccoli

- Cauliflower

- Sweet potato

- Zucchini

- Brussels sprouts

- Leafy greens such as spinach and kale

- Nuts (almonds, macadamia, Brazilian and walnuts)

- Raspberry and blackberry

- Chia and flax seeds

When you finally reach ketosis, you should have enough energy so that you can train with a minimal amount of carbohydrates from your diet.

But if you do not have enough fast carbohydrates, you should try using MCT oil, as it is an easily accessible source of energy. The MCT is easily digested, so you can use it without worrying about your sudden recovery.

5. Optimize your carbs

Of course, all people have different organic natures and a single approach is not desirable; but you can follow the following recommendations:

• It is best to avoid carbohydrates in the morning and choose MCT keto-coffee or a protein-rich breakfast instead.

• As for carbs for the rest of your day or evening, it depends on what you are going to do with them. Most people have enough fat to use as energy when they are in ketosis and perform light and moderate exercises.

6 Drink water.

It is also necessary to drink a sufficient amount of water - 2-2.5 liters per day. This helps restore balance in the body and avoid many difficulties when adapting the body to a new mode of operation.

How to Detect Ketosis

You can measure whether you are in a ketosis state with unique test strips that take urine or blood samples.

Instead of test strips, you can use this short list of physical symptoms that usually tell you if you are on the right track:

- **Increased urination**. Keto is like a natural diuretic drug, so you will feel the need to go to the toilet more. During urination, acetoacetate, a ketone body, is removed from the collection, which can increase the number of toilet visits.

- **Dry mouth**. Increased urination leads to dry mouth and increased thirst. It is necessary to make sure that you drink plenty of water and replenish electrolytes (salt, potassium, magnesium).

- **Bad breath.** Acetone is a ketone body that has a property that is partially excreted in your breath. It may smell like overripe fruit or as a nail polish remover. Usually, this is a temporary phenomenon that will soon pass. For more information on how to remove the smell from the mouth during keto, you can find out in this article.

- **Your hunger will decrease and your energy will increase**. As a rule, after you overcome the "keto-flu" (adaptation period), the feeling of hunger and tension will leave you.

Phases of a Proper Keto Diet

What happens to your body before ketosis?

For your body to adapt to the restriction of carbohydrates, it must undergo many changes. To better understand what is going on, let's break the path to ketosis into phases.

Phase 1 - Phase glycogen depletion - 6-24 hours after the start of the Ketogenic diet.

At this stage, most of the energy is provided by glycogen. Due to the lack of dietary carbohydrates, insulin levels begin to fall, with the result that water and sodium are excreted through the urine in much larger quantities. Some people may experience symptoms of mild dehydration, such as dizziness and fatigue.

Phase 2 - Gluconeogenic phase - from 2 to 10 days on a Ketogenic diet.

At this phase, glycogen is depleted; therefore, gluconeogenesis assumes the role of an energy source. At the moment, so much water and sodium are lost in the body that many people experience flu symptoms. The time window for this phase is so large (from two to ten days) because it depends on many factors of genetics and lifestyle.

Phase 3 - Ketosis Phase - 3 to 10 days on a Ketogenic diet.

During this phase, occurrence is characterized by a decrease in the breakdown of protein for energy and an increase in the consumption of fats and ketones. At this stage, ketones can provide up to 50% of your basic energy needs and 70% of your brain energy needs. Depending on the many factors of genetics and lifestyle, it can take you 3 to 10 days to get to this stage.

Keto flu: How to Prepare for This?

As soon as you eliminate carbohydrates from your diet, your body switches to a new source of energy, and it is not so easy. What can you expect? headache, nausea, dizziness, lack of strength and motivation, weakness, poor sleep, lethargy. Personally, all of the above may happen to you, or maybe just a few of the symptoms.

How long to last: from 2 days to 10 days, everything is very individual.

Adaptation to keto is the most challenging time; it is at this awkward moment that many people give up on all the positive qualities of this food system and say to themselves: "Why the hell am I torturing my precious body so much?... Burn it all down!!! Give me pasta, bread, and chocolate cake - I urgently need glucose!!!"

Well, wimps will stop reading right about now, while those committed to their own health and vitality will continue to read.

What to do to alleviate suffering:

1. Drink a lot of water (with the addition of a little lemon or salt), do not think and do not be horrified when you realize that 3-5 liters are consumed. Water helps the processes of the kidneys, which at first will get rid of the excess liquid, and in turn it will be kept by those carbohydrates.

2. Be sure to pre-stock up on a multi-vitamin complex and separately calcium, magnesium, potassium, and sodium - these guys will always be needed, always!!! With sodium, everything is clear - do not forget to salt the food. Total 3 jars, repeat:

1) a complex of vitamins

2) complex magnesium + calcium

3) potassium.

At the end of this book, I will share my shopping cart for these supplements.

3. Types of physical activity.

Long walks. It will help reduce cortisol levels, calm down insulin, and help to distract from naughty thoughts about sweets. Everything else will come with time, like jogging, strength training, and other workout routines. While you are adapting to ketosis, do not burden your body with a lot of exercises. Additional stress can throw you out of ketosis.

4. Buy kitchen scales or dust off those that have long been standing in the closet - now they are your best friends.

5. Download any convenient app for calorie counting.

6. Find a suitable and patient friend at this stage, who you can cry and complain to about how difficult it is to switch to the Keto Diet, but they will come to your house to collect all the bread, cakes, buckwheat, rice, and fruits, and they should encourage you and say: "You are strong; you can do everything !!! This is temporary!!!

You have so much waiting ahead! You will not feel hungry!

Doing calorie counts will make you lose weight! If you choose keto as a food system, generally, you will become more physically attractive.

After going through the "keto-flu", you feel like a superhero, and know how to make ketones, but your body needs time to thoroughly learn how to work with them and set up all the transport processes. After all, most of us have not got off the "glucose needle" since infancy.

A full-fledged adaptation may take several months, but you will hardly notice the changes - they will be internal. After that, you will be a fully "keto-adapted" person.

To summarize: prepare for this process, do not do everything carelessly! It is your attitude and your desire to be healthy and beautiful that will allow you to go through this process faster and less painfully!

P.S. By the way, the first minimum period is 2 weeks. During this time period you should ingest only keto friendly items.

What is Intermittent Fasting?

Finally, we get to fasting!

Before we introduce you to this, let's focus on two points:

1) If you are on a Ketogenic diet, but not yet in deep ketosis, i.e., you have a feeling of hunger - do not read further, set this aside for the future;

2) Interval fasting has nothing to do with calorie restriction. It is simply a reduction in the length of time during the day (interval) when you can eat. Usually without food spend from 14 to 20 hours a day.

So, several months of ketosis are over, and you are happy to feel the following manifestations of this state of the body: the absence of hunger as a concept, a reduction in the quantity and quality of sleep, an inexhaustible supply of energy, i.e., simple joys of keto; let's try to make an upgrade and go to the interval starvation. In other words, divide your day into two parts: the smaller, during which you eat; and the more significant, absolutely free from any food. I will try first to explain why, and then how to do it.

Without reference to any particular age, I can say that it is imperative to reduce insulin levels and increase the production of growth hormone. These two hormones are far from a complete list, but it is by their example that I will tell why we need interval starvation.

Insulin is produced in response to any food, which means we need to make part of your day free from its production. Because growth hormones are normally only created during lengthy periods of lowered insulin production.

HGH causes fresh and wrinkle-free skin, healthy joints, muscle tone, and of course a low percentage of fat. All these manifestations of its activity we lose over the years as production decreases. Interval fasting increases the production of growth hormone by 2000%.

If a previous couple of paragraphs answered the question "why?" For you, let's move on to the question "how?". First of all, being in ketosis, smoothly and, of course, without changing your current macros either in terms of ratio or total calories.

Step 1: Suppose you eat three times a day at a keto and make one or two snacks according to the habits acquired in childhood. Clear the intervals between meals of any calories. The challenge is to have only three flashes of insulin during the day. Suppose you put the first bite of food in your mouth at 7 am during breakfast, and the last one was swallowed at 8 pm during dinner. So, we have 13 + 11.

13 – hour food consumption period and an 11-hour food-free period. It is during these 11 hours that your insulin remains low, and the growth hormone can roam.

Step 2: We begin to squeeze our 13 hours and, accordingly, stretch our 11 hours. You can both postpone your breakfast an hour later, i.e., at 8 am, and eat your dinner an 8 pm
As a result, we get 12 + 12. Stay in this mode until you get used to it and then, reduce the meal period for another hour by switching to 11 + 13.

The frequency and size of your small steps are limited only by the adaptive abilities of your body.

Thus, sooner or later, you will come to 8 + 16. Within 8 hours, you eat up all your food in three doses (no snacking) and for the next 16 hours, you refrain from eating.

Step 3: Now you have two meals. What food intake you exclude is up to you. While not reducing calorie intake, what you ate for three meals, you eat in two. Stay in this mode until you get used to it and then, we begin to squeeze our 8-hour period to 4-hour gradually.

Thus, the time from the moment of the first piece put in the mouth, to the last swallowed one will be 4 hours, i.e., you will go to 4 + 20.

In conclusion, it is important to note that with the same caloric content and level of physical activity, the increased production of growth hormones will begin to reverse time and soon you will see traces of its work in the mirror.

One request; do not perform the steps described above too quickly, and listen to your body. Like the ketogenic diet, interval starvation should not bring the slightest discomfort.

Full Keto Diet Food List

Eat natural, high-quality, fresh food. Ideally, the food you buy should not even have an extensive list of ingredients.

A few words about snacks: they are not the best option. But in the first week, you can be more forgiving. Feel the need - keto food at your fingertips: nuts, cheese, keto fat bombs. Let's get rid of snacking eventually.

Below you will find several tables showing ketogenic products.

Table: Allowed Products

Category	Varieties
Animal products	Red and white meat - veal, pork, rabbit Bird - chicken, turkey, quail, duck Fatty fish - salmon, herring, tuna, trout, halibut, cod and catfish Eggs - Chicken, Quail

Milk products	Whole milk above 3% Cream 20-40% Sour cream from 20% Cottage cheese from 5% Hard cheeses from 45% Greek yogurt Kefir
Natural and vegetable fats	Lard and fat Butter, Coconut, Avocado, Flaxseed, Sunflower, Corn and Olive Oil
Mushrooms	All edible
Solanaceous and green vegetables (It is better to use those that grow above the ground).	All kinds of cabbage and salads, zucchini, asparagus, olives, cauliflower, Brussels sprouts, eggplant, green onions, celery, asparagus, any greens, bell pepper. Cucumbers, pumpkin, and tomatoes in moderation
Nuts and seeds	macadamia, walnuts, pecans, Brazil nuts, hazelnuts, pine nuts, almonds, cashews and pistachios.

	Seeds of pumpkin, sesame, sunflower, chia, flax, hemp
Organic drinks	Pure water. Water with slices of fruits or cucumbers
	Water with 1-2 drops of lemon or lime juice
	Bone broth (improves immunity and intestinal health)
	Black or green tea
	Coffee with heavy cream or coconut milk
	Unsweetened almond or hemp milk

Table: Prohibited Products

Category	Varieties	Exceptions
Sugar, sweeteners and sugar products	Candy, confectionery Sweet drinks, fruit juices, energy, soda White and milk chocolate, ice cream Breakfast cereals	Dark chocolate over 70% cocoa and in moderation
Starchy and flour products	Bread, pastries, pasta, potatoes, whole grains, cereals, beans	Chickpeas, brown rice in small quantities, toasts, bread
Alcoholic drinks	Beer, tinctures and sweet liquors	Dry wines, unsweetened strong drinks - vodka, whiskey, rum, gin, unsweetened cocktails
Fruits and	Bananas, strawberries,	Avocado,

dried fruits, sweet berries	cherries, apricots, peaches, pears, grapes, nectarines	Coconut, Sour Apples, Citrus Sour berries - raspberries, blueberries, cherries, cranberries and blackberries

Replacing familiar products with keto-friendly

Instead	Use
Sugar	**Stevia -** This is an excellent additional sweetener during the keto diet, which can even have a positive health effect. **Erythrol -** It is almost completely excreted through the urine and causes a very slight gastric upset. Although it may have a slight aftertaste, in combination with other sweeteners this is not very noticeable. **Xylitol -** Use carefully. Although it is an excellent sweetener and can be used to almost completely replace sugar, it can cause stomach discomfort when overeating. **monk fruit -** Asian fruit, contains a large amount of antioxidants, is used in traditional Chinese medicine. It is difficult to find in its pure form. It is 300 times sweeter than sugar!
Rice	Cauliflower
Flour	Walnut flour: almonds, coconut Flax Seed Flour Psyllium - used in baking to add texture to the dough
Thickener	Gum: guar and xanthan

Pasta	Zucchini and Shirataki noodles (a natural product that contains almost no calories, consists of dietary fiber, and is recommended for people who care about their health, control body weight, as well as blood sugar).
potatoes	Fried radish, celery root, kohlrabi, turnip
milk	Vegetable milk from hemp, almond and coconut seeds

Chapter 3 - Tips for Successfully Passing Keto

Four Quick Ways to Return to Ketosis.

The situation described in this article is more than typical. You interrupted the state of ketosis while on a trip or staged yourself a cheat meal - it is not so important what it was. We will look at the four fastest ways to return to the state of ketosis.

1. Include in your next workout in the exercise room, the upper body and the lower. I know that you usually do not do that, but now it's worth it.

By alternating exercises to the top and bottom of the body, we more effectively help our lymphatic system.

The lymphatic system is entirely separate from the circulatory system. It is a network of vessels running throughout the body. It carries white blood bodies, some proteins, and very few red blood bodies. The main task is to supply the body with essential substances and vice versa, and also to remove toxins. How does this relate to ketosis? Lymph nodes transport fatty acids. Fats travel through the lymphatic system even before they enter the circulatory system. In contrast to the blood that the heart drives through the vessels, the lymph moves through the lymphatic vessels only due to the reduction of skeletal muscles and that is why we need to do exercises on different parts of the body in one workout. Thus, we literally drive fats all over the body in the lymph and they get into the liver faster, converting to ketones and returning us to ketosis faster.

2. Caffeine. Increasing the caffeine dose during this period is guaranteed to increase the number of ketones produced. However, it is still necessary to exercise caution and moderation in using this method to return to ketosis, and not to go through a dose of caffeine.

3. MCT oil. Why is it worth to double your usual dose of MCT oil for a speedy return to ketosis? Because this oil does not have to pass through the liver to participate in the ketone production process. Usually, they consume fat through the entire cleavage path and then get into the liver. *MCT oil from the digestive system is immediately sent to the bloodstream, bypassing the liver, and is instantly used in mitochondria.*

4. It is unlikely to suit beginners - fasting. In the process of fasting, your body produces the hormone glucagon, which causes the body to utilize all the glycogen to the maximum. So, glycogen is used, and the body starts to produce ketones at an accelerated rate. It must be admitted that in this case, the muscles will be partially split to obtain nutrients but in small quantities.

All of the above methods will help you to quickly return to ketosis and the first three of them can be used by beginners for the initial entry into it.

Major Mistakes.

There are many mistakes for beginners, so let's proceed in an orderly fashion.

1. The Ketogenic Diet, is considered a diet, because it contains specific rules and is used for therapeutic purposes. However, this is where its similarity with dieting ends. Having understood and mastered keto, you will see that it is fundamentally wrong to apply any time frame to this process. Once you go into ketosis, you take advantage of this state of the body and notice that with each month of being in ketosis there are more and more decisive moments and they become more pronounced. In other words, it is not necessary to practice keto from one carbohydrate load to another. It is the continuity of being in ketosis that is the main idea of keto, as a way of life.

2. Inherent power. It's easy to understand the point of view of the supporters of intuitive nutrition - not to consider macros as much more comfortable than conducting a daily analysis of food eaten and, moreover, to plan tomorrow's diet. The proportions of macros are not empty figures at all, and following them will save you from many unpleasant moments and bring you closer to achieving your goals. It's not hard to check the truth of these words – after two weeks eating in strict accordance with Keto proportions and your calculated number of calories, you will become a staunch supporter of this approach.

3. Neglect of ketosis caused by the condition of microelement doses: the body's need for potassium, magnesium, sodium, calcium is very different from any other modes of your body. Spend some time with this issue, and little problems with well-being will disappear.

4. Unlimited food intake, even in full accordance with keto proportions, and supported by well-chosen composition and number of trace elements. The essence of keto is to force the body to use its fat reserves as an energy source. Turning to keto, you made a big step in this direction: you got rid of the feeling of hunger, transferred energy supply from glucose to ketones, but until you consume an excess of calories, your body will not consider your body fat as an energy source.

Having understood these 4 points once and for all, it will be much easier for you to proceed to the process of "tweaking" your food with keto.

I repeat once more: do not be lazy, pay attention to yourself; communicate with yourself, listen to yourself, and everything will work out!!!

Frequently Asked Questions About the Keto Diet

Will I eat carbohydrates? In general, yes. The main thing is to significantly reduce consumption in the first weeks to adapt to the body. Then you can increase use.

Does non-keto muscle loss occur? There is a risk of losing a small amount of muscle, but with proper intake of enough protein, the problem is solved.

Is it possible to gain muscle mass on the keto diet? Yes, but the technique will be very different from the usual weight gain, both in exercise and in the diet.

Do you need carbohydrate loading? In general, it is not recommended. The exception is intense training with going beyond the anaerobic threshold for weight gain.

How much should you eat of protein? It is not recommended to count in percent. Protein should be from 0.7 to 1.2 grams per 1 kilogram of desired weight.

What if I feel constant fatigue and fatigue on keto diet? This is the initial stage, and most likely the transition to ketosis, when the adaptation of the body to it is not completed. Watch for carbohydrates, maybe temporarily reduce their amount, and add more MCT oil (coconut Extra Virgin).

Urine begins to smell strange? The body has passed into ketosis; everything is fine, continue.

They say that ketosis is dangerous to health, is that so? Ketosis and ketoacidosis are often confused. These are different processes. Ketoacidosis is possible only in diabetic patients who do not control their condition. Ketosis is a natural and healthy state.

After the start of the Keto Diet, and problems began with stools, what should I do? This can happen during the restructuring of the body. Add fiber to your diet in the form of vegetables or as an additive. Bone broth with tissue will help.

What Supplements and Vitamins to Take on a Keto Diet.

Any diet is a restriction on the supply of certain nutrients. Keto diet in this regard is no exception. You almost wholly exclude carbohydrates from your diet, so it is highly desirable for you to use certain supplements and vitamins so that the body tolerates stress more efficiently. You can do without them, but if you want to be sure that you do not harm your health, then it is better to use at least the basic ones.

As promised, I am sharing with you the products that I use myself for the best results during Keto.

Basket №1 - the main set for a beginner https://iherb.co/LDCdqojS this includes a multivitamin complex explicitly adapted for men or women; calcium and magnesium in one bottle, potassium, omega 3, vitamin D.

Basket №2 - for advanced users https://iherb.co/FLFtwEaw Here we also have a vitamin complex explicitly adapted for men or women, calcium citrate, magnesium and potassium quotes.

Products that I buy here, I share my best practices with you https://iherb.co/D4uMBGcy

Chapter 4 - Keto Recipes Breakfasts

Low-Carb Sour Berry Cake

This original, delicious breakfast can satisfy you all morning. The cupcakes are the perfect way to energize your day.

Serves: 15

Prep time: 15 minutes

Cook time: 20 minutes

Ingredients:
- 2 cups of almond flour

- ½ tsp of baking soda

- ¼ cup of Erythritol

- 1 cup of sour cream

- ½ tsp of salt

- 2 eggs

- 4 ounces of blueberries, fresh

- 1/8 cup of butter, melted

Directions:

1. In the preheated oven 350 ° F (175 ° C), Place cupcake papers inside the individual muffin holes of your muffin tin.

2. Next, mix all the dry ingredients.

3. In another bowl, beat the eggs lightly. Add the butter and sour cream. Mix until thoroughly combined.

4. Combine the almond flour mixture with the sour cream mixture. Stir until thoroughly mixed. Add the blueberries until they are evenly incorporated.

5. Pour the resulting dough into forms paper up to ½ full.

6. Bake the muffins until golden, or for about 20 minutes.

7. Allow to slightly cool. Serve hot with butter.

Nutrients per serving:

- Carbs: 5 g

- Fat: 13 g

- Protein: 5 g

- Calories: 147 kcal

Coconut Breakfast Cereal

For those who rarely eat porridge, this recipe will give good taste. It will conquer you with its incredible coconut aroma and, unlike the usual coconut porridge, it is not high in carbohydrate, and this will make you like it more.

Servings: 4

Prep time: 10 minutes

Cook time: 30 minutes

Ingredients:

- 2 cup of water

- 1 cup of 36 percent heavy cream

- ½ tbsp. of unsweetened dried shredded coconut

- 2 tbsp. of flaxseed meal

- 1 tbsp. of butter

- 1½ tsp. of stevia

- 1 tsp. of cinnamon

- Sea salt

Directions:

1. We need to combine all the ingredients in a small pot, and mix well until smooth.
2. Put the pot over a medium-low flame and bring to a slow boil. Once boiling, stir well and remove from the heat.
3. Divide into four equal servings and set aside for 10 minutes to thicken. Best served warm. Store in mason jars, seal tightly and refrigerate for up to 2 days.

Nutritional:

- Calories: 171 kcal

- Fats: 16 g

- Net Carbs: 6 g

- Protein: 2 g

Vegetable Casserole

This dish turns out very tasty and tender; bright, and satisfying. Try to make a casserole from this recipe, and I am sure that it will surprise you with its excellent taste.

Servings: 3

Prep time: 10 minutes

Cook time: 30 minutes

Ingredients:

- 8 oz. of shredded mozzarella cheese

- 8 oz. of shredded cheddar cheese

- 6 large eggs

- 1 cup of cauliflower

- 4 tbsps. of butter

Directions:

1. Carefully mix the cheeses and eggs.
2. Butter the bottom of a skillet; add the cauliflower and the cheese mixture. Set oven to 350F, and bake for 35 minutes; then for 30 more minutes at 250 degrees F.
3. Serve

Nutrients per serving:

- Calories: 782kcal

- Fats: 62.6g

- Net Carbs: 4.4g

- Protein: 51.6g

Perfect Keto Pancakes

Quick and tasty! Pancakes are very tender and soft, in addition to being porous with a gently creamy taste.

Servings: 4

Prep time: 5 minutes

Cook time: 15 minutes

Ingredients:

- 4 tsp. of maple extract
- 2 oz (60 g) of almond flour
- 8 eggs
- 4 tsp. Of cinnamon

- 8 tbsp. of coconut oil
- 2 ¾ oz. pork rinds

Directions:

1. Grind pork rinds in a blender. Then add everything to the rest of the ingredients and mix them until smooth.
2. Heat a skillet to medium (300-400°F) and add the coconut oil into it.
3. Pour batter into the skillet, fry it until golden brown (around 2 minutes), and of course, don't forget to flip it!
4. Bonus: If you want a sweet finish, you can add some fruit (for example strawberries) to it.

Nutrients per serving:

- Calories: 510 kcal
- Fat: 43 g
- Carbs: 2 g
- Protein: 24 g

Egg Muffins with Broccoli for Breakfast

An excellent start for a new day can be a delicious breakfast; for example, egg muffins with broccoli.

Servings: 4

Prep time: 10 minutes

Cook time: 30 minutes

Ingredients:

- 2 tsp of ghee, soft

- 2 eggs

- 2 cups of almond flour

- 1 cup of broccoli florets, chopped

- 1 cup of almond milk

- 1 tsp of baking powder

- salt, pepper to taste

Directions:

1. In a bowl, mix the eggs with the flour, broccoli, milk, yeast and baking powder, and stir really well.
2. Grease a muffin tray with the ghee; divide broccoli mix, put them in the oven and cook at 350 degrees F for 30 minutes.
3. Serve these muffins for breakfast.

Nutrients per serving:

- Calories: 204 kcal

- Fat: 4 g

- Carbs: 15 g

- Protein: 11 g

Seafood Omelet

So, you love Seafood? An omelet is undoubtedly the best option for breakfast, and adding seafood to it makes it very tasty and unique.

Servings: 4

Prep time: 5 minutes

Cook time: 15 minutes

Ingredients:

- 12 eggs

- 4 garlic cloves

- 1 cup of mayonnaise (of course you can lower it according to your taste)

- 2 red chili peppers

- 10 oz. Of boiled shrimp or some seafood mix

- 4 tbsp. Of olive oil

- chives

- 4 tbs. of olive oil/butter

- salt and pepper to your taste

Directions:

1. Heat the frying pan, and fry seafood, garlic, and chili in olive oil; add salt and pepper to taste. Then set it aside and cool to room temperature.
2. Add the chives (optional) and mayo to the cooled mixture.
3. Whisk the eggs together, season them, and fry them in a skillet.
4. Add the mix. When your omelet is almost ready, fold it, lower the temperature a bit, and let it set completely. Serve it immediately for the best taste.

Nutrients per serving:

- Calories: 872 kcal

- Fat: 83 g

- Carbs: 4 g

- Protein: 27 g

Salad Sandwich

Yes, in the keto diet, this sandwich without bread option is also possible! Pretty cool, huh? Anyway, this easy meal is perfect for the morning, so you can pack it to work as a fast lunch or as a snack!

Servings: 1

Prep time:5-10 minutes based on the amount you will make

Cook time:5-10 minutes

Ingredients:

- 2 oz. of lettuce

- ½ avocado

- 1 cherry tomato

- 1 oz. of Edam cheese (or any cheese you prefer)

- ½ oz. of butter

Directions:

1. Rinse and cut the lettuce. Then use it as the base of your sandwich.
2. Cover the leaves with butter and place the cheese, avocado, and tomato on top of it.
3. Extra: If you want to add something more to your sandwich, try to place some eggs on the top of everything.

Nutrients per serving:

- Calories: 419 kcal

- Fat: 43 g

- Carbs: 4 g

- Protein: 4 g

Ground Beef and Creamy Cauliflower Made in a Skillet

This dish is colorful for its taste and it is incredibly satisfying. This one will fill your stomach to the max, we promise you!

Servings: 4

Prep time: 5 minutes

Cook time: 25 minutes

Ingredients:

- 2 cloves of garlic chopped

- 4 jalapeno peppers

- 2 tbsps. of ghee

- ½ cup of water

- 1 head cauliflower (1 lb)

- 1 lb lean ground beef

- 1 onion

- Salt

- Pepper

- 4 tbsps. of mayo

- 4 eggs

- 1 tbsp. of fresh parsley

- ½ ripe avocado

Directions:

1. Melt the ghee in your skillet around 300-400 °F (Medium-high). When it's beautiful and hot, add the onion, garlic, and jalapeno. Cook it until softened (around 2-3 minutes).

2. Add the ground beef, and season it with salt and pepper. Continue applying the heat until the meat becomes completely brown. Then lower the heat to 200-300 °F (Medium-low), add the cauliflower, and continue for 2-3 minutes.

3. Then add water. Continue with Step 2 for 3-5 mins, until the liquids are absorbed.

4. Mix eggs, mayonnaise, and greens; salt to taste and pour this mixture in a pan with minced meat.

5. Cook under the closed lid until ready in 5-10 minutes

6. Then garnish it with the diced avocado and the chopped parsley.

Nutrients per serving:

- Calories: 688 kcal

- Fat: 52 g

- Protein: 38 g

- Carbs: 14 g

Awesome Breakfast Salad

A refreshing hearty salad, and the best start to a new day.

Servings: 2

Prep time: 3 minutes

Cook time: 15 minutes

Ingredients:

- 2 eggs

- 2 ozs. of avocado (sliced preferred)

- 4 strips of bacon

77

- Black pepper, salt

- 1 tsp. of red wine vinegar

- 2 tsp. of virgin olive oil

- 3 shredded Lacinto kale

Directions:

1. Use a bowl to combine the kale, olive oil, vinegar, and a bit of salt. Smash them with your hands until the kale softens a bit.
2. Cook the eggs to suit your style (medium boiled recommended here), and cook your bacon.
3. Divide it into 2 plates. Use your toppings, the bacon, and avocado for your desired outcome, and don't forget to season it.

Nutrients per serving:

- Calories: 292 kcal

- Fats: 18 g

- Carbs: 8 g

- Protein: 18 g

Boiled Eggs with Mayo

This Keto diet is like magic for egg lovers! It is a versatile dish adored by adults and children. It is prepared quickly and combined with many different ingredients.

Servings: 4

Prep time:3 minutes

Cook time:10 minutes

Ingredients:

- 8 eggs

- 8 tbsps. of mayo

- Avocado (optional, but recommended)

Directions:

1. Boil water in a pot, and carefully put the eggs in the water
2. Boil the eggs: 5-6 mins. for soft, 6-8 mins. for medium, 8-10 mins. for hard-boiled eggs.
3. Tip: Serve it simple with the mayo and the avocado. Another option is to mash together the mayo and avocado. Alternatively, you can mix everything by smashing the eggs into the mixture, and creating a delicious cream.

Nutrients per serving:

- Calories: 316 kcal

- Fat: 29 g

- Carbs: 1 g

- Protein: 11 g

Eggs in Nests

Want an original breakfast? Be sure to try this dish; it has excellent taste!

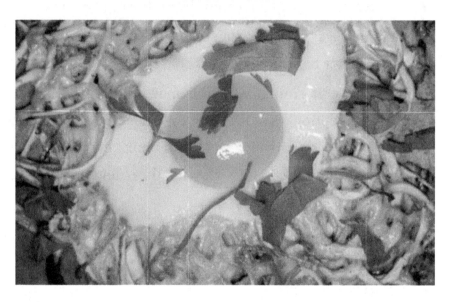

Servings: 4

Prep time: 10 minutes

Cook time: 30 minutes

Ingredients:

- 8 oz. of grated zucchini

- 4 tsp. of butter

- ¼ tsp. of sea salt

- ½ tsp. of Black pepper

- ½ tsp. of Paprika

- 4 eggs

- 4 oz. of shredded cheddar cheese

- 4 ramekins

Directions:

1. Preheat the Air Fryer at 356°F.
2. Grate the zucchini. Add the butter to the ramekins and add the zucchini in a nest shape. Sprinkle with the paprika, salt, and pepper.
3. Whisk the eggs and add to the nest, topping it off with the cheese.
4. Air fry for 7 minutes. Chill for 3 minutes and serve in the ramekin.

Nutrients per serving:

- Calories: 221kcal

- Fat: 17.7g

- Protein: 13.4g

- Carbs: 2.9g

Cauliflower Fritters

An excellent recipe for vegetable pancakes will surprise you. Dedicated to all cauliflower lovers! You can serve as a separate dish with sour cream, or as a side dish. Gentle, airy, and very tasty!

Servings: 2
Prep time: 10 minutes
Cook time: 15 minutes

Ingredients:

- 2 eggs

- 1 head of cauliflower

- 1 tbsp. of yeast

- Sea salt, black pepper

- 1-2 tbsp. of ghee

- 1 tbsp. of turmeric

- 2/3 cup of almond flour

Directions:

1. Cook the cauliflower in a large saucepan for 8 minutes.
2. Add the eggs, almond flour, yeast, turmeric, salt and pepper to a mixing bowl. Stir well. Form into patties.
3. Heat your ghee to medium in a skillet. Form your fritters and cook until golden on each side (3-4 mins).
4. Serve it while hot.

Nutrients per serving:

- Calories: 238 kcal

- Fat: 23 g

- Carbs: 5 g

- Protein: 6 g

Bulletproof Coffee

In taste, this drink is like a creamy latte but does not contain sugar or milk. As for the effect, it does not only invigorates and improves cognitive functions, it also helps to improve metabolism and reduce cholesterol.

Servings: 1

Prep time: 5 minutes

Cook time: 10 minutes

Ingredients:

- 1 cup of water
- 2 tbsp of coffee
- 1 tbsp of grass fed butter
- 1 tbsp of coconut oil
- ¼ tsp of vanilla extract

Directions:

1. Make coffee to your taste.
2. Add the coffee, butter and coconut oil to the blender.
3. Add the vanilla extract and a pinch of cinnamon; blend for 20 seconds.

Nutrients per serving:

- Calories: 284 kcal
- Fat: 24.43g
- Carbs: 0.14g
- Protein: 16.54g

Stuffed Avocado

This recipe is made for those days when the morning is heavy, you are late, and you need to cook something quickly!

Servings: 1

Prep time: 5 minutes

Cook time: 15 minutes

Ingredients:

- 1 ripe avocado

- salt

- 1 lemon (the juice part of it)

- 1 oz. of goat cheese

- 2 ozs. of smoked salmon

Directions:

1. Cut the avocado, and remove the seed.
2. Mix the remaining ingredients, until they fuse well.
3. Place the cream inside the avocado.

Tip: If you want small snacks, you can cut the avocado into small pieces and serve it that way.

Nutrients per serving:

- Calories: 471 kcal

- Fat: 41 g

- Carbs: 4 g

- Protein: 19 g

Chapter 5: Lunch Recipes

Citrus Tilapia

The fish is incredibly tender, juicy, and easily digestible. It turned out a beautiful dish that is well suited for both weekdays and holidays. Help yourself!

Serves: 4
Prep time: 10 minutes
Cook time: 30 minutes

Ingredients:

- 4 tilapia fillets

- 2 garlic cloves, minced

- 2 tbsp of butter, melted

- 5 oz (150g) Cream 35% (fatty)

- 1 avocado

- Juice of 1 lemon

- Salt and pepper, to taste

- 2 tsp of chopped parsley

Directions:

1. Wash and clean the tilapia.
2. Preheat the oven to 375 °F.
3. In a bowl, mix cream, lemon juice, butter, garlic, parsley, salt, and pepper.
4. Layout the tilapia fillets in a baking dish.
5. Pour the sauce over tilapia.
6. Bake for 30 minutes.
7. Serve with avocado or steamed asparagus.

Nutrients per serving:

- Calories: 173 kcal

- Fat: 7.81g

- Carbs: 2.3g

- Protein: 16.69g

Baked Cauliflower with Cheese

The preparation of the dish is straightforward. It requires a small amount of ingredients and, most importantly, it is prepared very quickly!
You can use cauliflower in large quantities without being afraid of gaining weight. This valuable diet product also has a unique taste. Cauliflower can be used both fresh and frozen.

Servings: 4
Prep time: 15 minutes
Cook time: 35 minutes

Ingredients:
- 1 head of cauliflower, cut into florets

- 1 cup of heavy cream

- Sliced bacon, cooked

- 1/2 cup of shredded cheddar cheese

- ¼ cup of chopped green onions

- 2 oz. of cream cheese

- 2 tbsps. of butter

- Salt and pepper

Directions:

1. Preheat your oven to 350°F.
2. Boil water, and cook your florets for 2 minutes. Drain them after.
3. In a pot, melt the butter, heavy cream, cream cheese, half of the cheddar cheese and season it after being thoroughly combined.
4. In a baking dish, mix everything; all except a bit of bacon, green onions, and the rest of the cheddar.
5. Use those to top your meal.
6. Bake until golden; around 25-30 minutes.

Nutrients per serving:

- Calories: 498 kcal

- Fat: 45 g

- Carbs: 6 g

- Protein: 14 g

Keto "Fried" Chicken

I think everyone should learn this recipe for making delicious chicken in a pan; it's no wonder they say that everything ingenious is simple! So here is it - simple ingredients, but so tasty!

Servings: 4
Prep time: 15 minutes
Cook time: 40 minutes

Ingredients:

- 1 pound (6-8) skinless chicken thighs

- 1 cup of sunflower seeds

- ½ cup of sesame seeds

- 2 tbsps. of avocado oil

- 1 tsp of salt, pepper, Italian herbs

Directions:

1. Preheat your oven to 425 °F. Grease a pan with the oil.
2. Put the seeds and the season in a blender. Grind until you have a beautiful texture.
3. Add the mix to a freezer bag; then add a chicken thigh to the bag, and shake it up until well-coated. Repeat with all chicken.
4. Roast it for 30 minutes, turning them at half of the total directions' time.

Nutrients per serving:

- Calories: 340 kcal

- Fats: 33 g

- Carbs: 7 g

- Protein: 14 g

Goat Cheese Omelet

I learned how to cook a delicious omelet with goat cheese on vacation, in a small private cafe. An inexperienced chef can easily handle a simple recipe of food with goat cheese!

Serves: 4
Prep time: 15 minutes
Cook time: 15 minutes

Ingredients:
- 8 large eggs

- 2 tbsp of butter

- 2 tsp of olive oil

- 1 tsp of Dijon mustard

- 6 cups of spinach

- 8 oz. of goat cheese

- 4 tbsp of heavy cream

- ¼ cup of scallions, chopped

- Ground pepper and salt to taste

Directions:

1. In a pan, heat 2 tsp of olive oil.
2. Add the spinach and sauté for one to two minutes. Add the mustard, pepper, and salt.
3. Remove vegetables from the pan. Set aside.
4. Mix 8 large eggs, cream, salt, and pepper in a large bowl.
5. Now, take the egg mixture and pour it into a preheated pan with melted butter. Cook for about one minute. You may need to cook in 2 or more batches.
6. Spoon spinach and crumble goat cheese over the eggs.
7. Cook for another 2-3 minutes.
8. Fold the omelet.
9. Garnish with the scallions.

Nutrients per serving:

- Calories: 506 kcal

- Fat: 43.01g

- Carbs: 4.7g

- Protein: 24.74g

Chicken with Vegetables

This low-calorie and healthy dish is a favorite in our family. It is prepared in two accounts. Vitamins in it - do not count; at the same time, it looks very beautiful on a plate. Recommended!

Servings: 2

Prep time: 10 minutes

Cook time: 20 minutes

Ingredients:

- 1 boneless, skinless chicken thighs

- 2 garlic cloves

- 6-8 lettuce leaves

- ¼ cup of minced onion

- ¼ cup of broccoli

- ¼ cup of sour cream

- 2 tsp. of curry powder

- 3 tbsps. of ghee

- Salt, black pepper

Directions:

1. Prepare your veggies and cut your chicken thighs.
2. Heat a skillet on medium heat. When it reaches the temperature, add the ghee, broccoli, and the onion.
3. Add the chicken while seasoning it. Cook it while frequently stirring for about 8 mins.
4. Add in the curry. Sauté until well-combined.
5. Layout your leaves; place the mix inside them, and roll them up. Top with the sour cream.

Nutrients per serving:

- Calories: 554 kcal

- Fat: 36 g

- Carbs: 7 g

- Protein: 41 g

Keto Meatloaf

The meat casserole prepared in this way is very juicy and very tasty. Once you cook it once, this meatloaf will become a favorite in your kitchen. Best served hot. Enjoy your meal!

Servings: 6

Prepare time: 10 minutes

Directions time: 50 minutes

Ingredients:

- 2 lb of lean ground beef

- 2 eggs

- 4 cloves garlic

- ¼ cup of chopped oregano

- ¼ chopped parsley

- ½ tbsp. of salt and pepper

- 1 tbsp. of lemon zest

- 2 tbsps. of avocado oil

Directions:

1. Preheat your oven to 400°F
2. In a bowl, mix your beef, salt, and pepper.
3. In a blender, stir the eggs, oil, herbs, and garlic. Blend until looking fluffy. Combine your 2 mixtures.
4. Add it to a small loaf pan and then flatten it out.
5. Set in the oven for 50 mins.
6. Garnish it with lemon after letting it cool.

Nutrients per serving:

- Calories: 344 kcal

- Fat: 29 g

- Carbs: 4 g

- Protein: 33 g

Chicken with Mushrooms in a Creamy Sauce

This is one of those dishes that are prepared quite naturally, but they turn out to be amazingly tasty. Tender and juicy chicken meat combined with mushrooms and cream sauce, is great for lunch.

Servings: 2
Prep time: 5 minutes
Cook time: 25 minutes

Ingredients:

- 5 cremini mushrooms

- 2 chicken breast

- 1 onion

- ½ tsp. of dried thyme

- 3 tbsps.of butter

- 1/3 cup of fat canned coconut milk

- Salt and pepper

Directions:

1. Heat your skillet to medium heat. Slice up your mushrooms and onion.

2. Once it's hot, add the butter. When melted, add in the mushrooms and a bit of salt. Sauté until brown; then it's the onion's turn. Keep stirring for 6 minutes and then remove the mix.

3. Add the remaining butter and melt it. Sprinkle chicken fillet with salt, pepper, and thyme, and then place it in the skillet. Cook each side for 5 mins. Finally, place your mix back, pour the coconut milk right over it, and cook for 15 minutes

Nutrients per serving:
- Calories: 334 kcal

- Fat: 27 g

- Carbs: 3 g

- Protein: 24 g

Keto Lasagna

This amazing lasagna does not have flour and it is great for the keto diet. Thin cabbage leaves are also suitable instead of zucchini; do not be afraid of experimentation!

Servings: 6
Prep time: 10 minutes
Cook time: 40 minutes

Ingredients:

- ½ lb. of ground beef

- 1 egg

- 1 clove garlic (chopped)

- 4 large zucchinis

- 16 ozs. of marinara sauce

- 1 tbsp. of butter or coconut oil

- 2 tbsps.of coconut flour

- 1 tbsp. of Italian herb

- salt and pepper

- 1 tsp. of garlic powder

- 1 ½ mozzarella

- ½ cup of parmesan

- ½ tsp. of red pepper for spice

- ¼ cup of basil

Directions:

1. Slice the zucchini and season it. Then leave them for 30 minutes on a paper towel to extract any moisture.

2. Heat your butter or coconut oil in a large skillet over medium-high heat. Fry until it becomes ready ground beef.

3. Preheat your oven to 375 °F and coat a 9x9 baking dish with butter.

4. In a bowl, mix all your remaining ingredients until smooth, and set aside. Add the seasoning and red pepper to spice things up.

5. Make layers using your zucchini and then your mixture, up to 3-4 times. Finish with a layer of sauce.

6. Cover it up and bake for 20 minutes. Then remove the foil, and bake for another 15 minutes.

Nutrients per serving:

- Calories: 364 kcal

- Fat: 21 g

- Carbs: 8 g

- Protein: 32 g

Baked Salmon with Lemon

What could be more straightforward and tastier than baked redfish? I propose to see how to cook salmon, baked in the oven. Simple and amazingly delicious dish. Let's cook!

Servings: 6

Prep time: 10 minutes

Cook time: 25 minutes

Ingredients:

- 2 lbs. of salmon

- 1 lemon

- 1 tbsp. of olive oil

- Salt and pepper

Directions:

1. Preheat the oven to 400°F.

2. Grease a baking dish with olive oil and then place the salmon with the skin-side down. Season it well, slice the lemon thinly, and top the fish with it.

3. Bake the mixture for 25 mins until it flakes easily with a fork. Season it with salt and pepper.

Nutrients per serving:

- Calories: 573 kcal

- Fats: 49 g

- Carbs: 1 g

- Protein: 31 g

Soup Egg and Lemon with Chicken

As a first course, soup has always been and will be the best option. Light soup energizes and nourishes. I want to tell you how to cook chicken soup with an egg for lunch. And it's easy to cook.

Servings: 4

Prep time: 5 minutes

Cook time: 30 minutes

Ingredients:

- 4 cups of beef broth/water

- ¾ lb. of cauliflower

- 1 lb. of boneless chicken thighs

- 1/3 lb. of butter

- 4 eggs

- 1 lemon

- 2 tbsps. of fresh parsley

- 1 bay leaf

- Salt and pepper

Directions:

1. Slice your chicken thinly, and then place in a saucepan while adding beef broth and bay leaf. Let the meat simmer for 10 mins before removing it along with the bay leaf.

2. Grate your cauliflower and place it in a saucepan. Add butter and boil for a few minutes.

3. Beat your eggs and lemon juice in a bowl, and season it.

4. Reduce the heat a bit and add the eggs, stirring continuously. Let it simmer, but don't boil.

5. Return the chicken. Decorate with greens.

Nutrients per serving:
- Calories: 582 kcal

- Carbs: 4 g

- Fats: 49 g

- Protein: 31 g

Zucchini Noodle Shrimp

An original and tasty dish that can be prepared not only for lunch but also for dinner. Easy and quick to cook, it has an unusual taste ... this dish will surely be pleasant to you!

Serves: 4

Prep time: 20 minutes

Cook time: 10 minutes

Ingredients:

- 2 tbsp of unsalted butter

- 1 lb of medium shrimp, shelled and deveined

- 2 cloves garlic, minced

- ½ tsp of red pepper flakes

121

- ¼ cup of chicken stock

- Juice of 1 lemon

- 4 medium zucchini, spiralized

- 2 tbsp of freshly grated Parmesan

- Chopped parsley, for garnish

Directions:

1. Preheat a large frying pan to medium temperature; melt the butter and fry, stirring constantly the flakes of garlic and red pepper for 1 minute.
2. Add shrimp. Cook for about 3 minutes.
3. Add chicken stock and lemon juice, and stir.
4. Add the zucchini noodles and cook, occasionally stirring, for 2 minutes.
5. Season with salt and pepper
6. Garnish with Parmesan and parsley.
7. Serve immediately.

Nutrients per serving:

- Calories: 162 kcal

- Fat: 7.45g

- Net Carbs: 4.91g

- Protein: 18.14g

Chapter 6: Dinner Recipes

Rissole in Bacon

What do you cook with minced meat? There is one beautiful, simple, and easy recipe. I will tell you how to prepare the chops in bacon. Such rissole is cooked easily and quickly!

Serves: 4
Prep time: 15 minutes
Cook time: 30 minutes

Ingredients:
- 1 lb. of ground beef

- 2 oz. of cheddar cheese

- 20 bacon slices

- 4 tbsp. of peanut butter

- 1 tsp. of garlic powder

- 1 tsp. of onion powder

- 1 tsp. of salt

- ½ tsp. of pepper

Directions:

1. Mix the ground beef and seasonings.
2. Divide the meat and form them into four patties with your hands.
3. Cook on the grill until done.
4. Add 1 tablespoon peanut butter and sprinkle cheese onto each cooked burger.
5. Wrap up your burger in the bacon. About 5 slices per patty.
6. Cook for about 20 minutes in the oven at 400°F until the bacon begins to brown or when it has reached your preferred texture.
7. Serve with lettuce, red onion, or any desired toppings.

Nutrition Facts per Serving:

- Calories: 850 kcal

- Fat: 67.8g

- Carbs: 8.13g

- Protein: 49.82g

Baked Zucchini with Cheese

This dish will appeal to all who are crazy about zucchini! This dish is low-calorie and nourishing at the same time. It is easy to prepare; see for yourself, and try.

Serves: 4
Prep time: 15 minutes
Cook time: 30 minutes

Ingredients:

- 2 tbsp. of butter

- 1 small onion, diced

- 2 cloves garlic, minced

- 2 medium zucchini, sliced

- 2 medium yellow squash, sliced

- 1 cup of heavy cream

- 1 ½ cups cheese of your choice, shredded

- Salt and pepper to taste.

Directions:

1. Preheat the oven to 350°F.
2. Melt butter in a skillet and sauté onions and garlic until they appear translucent.
3. Add the heavy cream and 1 cup of cheese.
4. Simmer until the sauce has thickened.
5. Grease a casserole dish.
6. Put the sliced zucchini and yellow squash in the casserole dish.
7. Gently pour the butter and cream mixture over the vegetables, and sprinkle the remaining ½ cup of cheese over the top.
8. Put in the oven for 30 minutes, or until the liquid has thickened and the top is golden brown.
9. Serve warm.

Nutrients per serving:

- Calories: 371 kcal

- Fat: 33.68g

- Carbs: 4.43g

- Protein: 13.3g

Chicken Breasts with Cheese and Spinach

As a hot dish for lunch, dinner, or a festive table, I want to advise a new option. Juicy greens, tender cheese fillet is surprisingly tasty and quite comfortable.

Servings: 4

Prep time: 25 minutes

Cook time: 15 minutes

Ingredients:

- 1 ½ lb. of chicken breasts

- 4 ozs. of cream cheese

- ¼ cup of frozen spinach

- ½ cup of mozzarella

- 4 oz. of artichoke hearts

- ¼ cup of Greek yogurt

- Salt and pepper

- 2 tbsps. of olive oil

Directions:

1. Pound the breasts, about 1 inch thick. Cut each chicken down the middle, but don't cut through it. Make a pocket for the filling: Season the chicken.

2. In a bowl, combine the Greek yogurt, mozzarella, cream cheese, artichoke, and spinach. Next, season it. Mix until well-combined.

3. Fill all breasts equally with your mixture.

4. In a skillet, over medium heat, add the oil and place your chicken. Cover the skillet and cook for 5-6 mins, turning the heat up in the last 1-2 mins.

Nutrients per serving:
- Calories: 288 kcal

- Fats: 18 g

131

- Carbs: 3 g

- Protein: 31 g

Burrito in the Salad Leaves with Turkey

I offer you a delicious version of turkey burrito in lettuce, which is ideal not only for dinner. Burrito cooks very quickly, and is eaten even faster! Help yourself!

Servings: 1

Prep time: 5 minutes

Cook time: 25 minutes

Ingredients:

- 1 head lettuce

- 4 slices of deli turkey, cooked

- 4 slices of bacon, cooked

- 1 Roma tomato, sliced

- 1 avocado, sliced

- ½ cup of mayo

- 1 tsp. of lemon juice

- 6 large basil leaves

- 1 garlic clove, chopped

- Salt and pepper

Directions:

1. For your dressing: combine your lemon juice, basil leaves, garlic clove, and half of your mayo in a food processor.

2. Layout 2 lettuce leaves and then one layer of turkey before adding your mayo. Lay the second turkey on it, followed by one bacon slice and some avocado and tomato. Season them to your taste.

3. Roll them up and enjoy. Served cold is the best way for them.

Nutrients per serving:

- Calories: 367 kcal

- Fats: 27 g

- Carbs: 19 g

- Protein: 13 g

Keto Sushi

Sometimes you want to treat yourself to delicious dishes from Asian countries. I recommend a recipe that will appease your taste buds, and will not require time for its preparation.

Servings: 2
Prep time: 15 minutes
Cook time: 10 minutes

Ingredients:

- 1.5 oz. of cream cheese

- 1 cup of cauliflower, chopped

- ½ avocado

- 2.5 oz (70 g) of redfish

- ¼ cup of cucumber, soy sauce

- 1 tbsp. of coconut oil

- 1 nori wrapper

Directions:

1. Cut up your cauliflower into florets and pulse with a food processor.
2. Heat your oil in a skillet and add in your cauliflower. Cook for 4-7 mins, then place in a bowl and set aside.
3. Slice up your avocado, cucumber, redfish, and cheese. Then set aside with your cauliflower.
4. Place an extended layer of plastic wrap and lay the nori wrapper on top of it.
5. Spread the contents of it. You can mix up the sheet if you desire, but the recommended order is this: avocado -> cream cheese -> cucumber, redfish
6. Slowly roll up the nori wrapper around the insides, while paying attention not to mess up the whole thing.
7. Cut into the desired number of pieces.

Nutrients per serving:

- Calories: 241 kcal

- Fats: 22 g

- Carbs: 9 g

- Protein: 3 g

Creamy Broccoli and Leek Soup

Soups are indispensable for a healthy lifestyle. At home, it is possible to prepare a restaurant menu dish. In confirmation of this recipe, here is how to make broccoli cream soup with cream and onions. The soup is delicious, with a delicate texture, and nutritious.

Servings: 4

Prep time: 5 minutes

Cook time: 25 minutes

Ingredients:

- 10 oz. of broccoli

- 1 leek

- 8 oz. of cream cheese

- 3 oz. of butter

- 3 cup of water

- 1 garlic clove

- ½ cup of fresh basil

- Salt and pepper

Directions:

1. Rinse the leek and chop both parts finely. Slice the broccoli thinly.

2. Place the veggies in a pot and cover with water and then season them. Boil the water until the broccoli softens.

3. Add the florets and garlic, while lowering the heat.

4. Add in the cheese, butter, pepper, and basil. Blend to the desired consistency: if too thick, use water; if you want to make it thicker, use a little bit of heavy cream.

Nutrients per serving:

- Calories: 451 kcal

- Fats: 37 g

- Protein: 10 g

- Carbs: 4 g

Chicken with Lemon and Garlic

The aroma of baked chicken with garlic and lemon will not leave anyone indifferent. Crisp, tender, and juicy meat - you will lick your fingers! And preparing chicken is easy!

Servings: 4
Prep time: 5 minutes
Cook time: 20 minutes

Ingredients:

- 4 boneless chicken thighs

- 2 garlic cloves minced

- Juice of 1 lemon

- ¼ tsp. of smoked paprika, red chili flakes, garlic powder

- 2 tsp. of Italian seasoning

- 1 tbsp. of heavy cream

- Fresh parsley

- ¼ small onion

- 1 tbsp. of olive oil

- 1½ tbsp. of butter

- Salt and pepper

Directions:

1. Season your chicken with all spices.
2. In a skillet, over medium heat, add the olive oil and cook for 5-6 mins on each side. Set aside on a plate.
3. Heat the skillet again and add in the butter. Add onion, garlic, and your lemon juice; stir. Season them with everything left. After that, stir in your heavy cream. Once the sauce has thickened up, add the chicken back to the pot.
4. Serve it with lemon slices.

Nutrients per serving:

- Calories: 279 kcal

- Fats: 15 g

- Carbs: 3 g

- Protein: 15 g

Crispy Zucchini Pancakes

Fritters turn out just great! Of course, they can be made for breakfast, but we prefer it as a side dish for dinner with sour cream or homemade mayonnaise. Enjoy your meal!

Servings: 12

Prep time: 5 minutes

Cook time: 30 minutes

Ingredients:

- 1 lb zucchini

- 2 pcs. of Green onions

- 1 egg

- 1/4 tsp of turmeric

- 1/2 tsp of Garlic powder

- ½ cup (50g) Cheese Cheddar

- 3 tbsp. of Spoons Coconut Flour

- 1/4 tsp of baking powder

- Salt pepper to taste

Directions:

1. Grate zucchini
2. You will add all ingredients except eggs. Stir.
3. The dough should be sticky, but not watery.
4. Spread the pan and roast on medium heat from both sides. Alternatively, put on parchment and bake in the oven for 20 minutes

Nutrients per serving:

- Calories: 45 kcal

- Fats: 3.4 g

- Carbs: 2.4 g

- Protein: 3.1 g

Cheesy Broccoli Soup

The direction for making broccoli soup is a simple task, but preparing a delicious broccoli cream soup is much more difficult. Let me tell you how to do it.

Serves: 4

Prep time: 10 minutes

Cook time: 15 minutes

Ingredients:

- 1 small onion, diced

- 2 cloves garlic, minced

- 4 cups of chicken broth

- 1 tbsp. of cream cheese

- ¼ cup of heavy whipping cream

- 3 cups of broccoli (trimmed)

- 1 cup of cheddar cheese, shredded

- Salt and pepper, as needed

Directions:

1. In a large pot, melt butter over medium high heat and sauté onion for 3-4 minutes.
2. Add garlic and sauté for another 1 minute.
3. Pour the chicken broth and broccoli in the pot.
4. Bring to a boil and then simmer for a few minutes.
5. Beat the contents of the pan with a blender.
6. Add the cream and cream cheese into the soup and mix well.
7. Stir in cheddar cheese.

Nutrients per serving:

- Calories: 185 kcal

- Fat: 14.1g

- Carbs: 4.3g

- Protein: 10.07g

Fried Minced Dinner with Zucchini and Pepper

A simple and tasty dinner without much money, time, and effort. Only 4 ingredients are needed: minced meat, zucchini, small onion, and pepper. Add spices. Everything is done in a frying pan literally, in two steps.

Servings: 3

Prep time: 5 minutes

Cook time: 30 minutes

Ingredients:

- 1 lb mince (any for your taste)
- 1 zucchini; peel, and dice

- 1 small onion, chopped
- 1 paprika, chopped
- 1 garlic clove (optional), chopped finely
- 1 tablespoon of any fat
- 1 tsp of Zira (optional)
- Salt, black and red pepper to taste

Directions:

1. Preheat pan and throw a piece of coconut oil into it (or the one you use).

2. Put the onion, and then the mince.

3. After 2-3 minutes, put the zucchini. Fry the mixture for about 3-4 minutes.

4. Add spices, garlic, and pepper. Fry until golden brown.

Nutrients per serving:

- Calories: 390.57 kcal
- Carbs: 38.4 g
- Fats: 30 g
- Protein: 25 g

Stuffed Chicken Peppers

Well and deliciously stuffed peppers. The stuffing is not done the way it is usually done with stuffed peppers. It has chicken, Greek yogurt and avocado.

Servings: 3

Prep time: 5 minutes

Cook time: 40 minutes

Ingredients:

- 3 peppers cut in half, and the seeds and membranes removed
- 7 oz (200 g) boiled chicken breast cut into cubes
- 1 small white onion, chopped finely

- 1 avocado, cut into cubes
- 1 garlic clove (optional), chopped finely
- 1 tbsp lime juice
- 2/3 (140 g) Greek yogurt
- 1 hot pepper, chopped finely
- 1 oz fresh cilantro, chopped finely
- Salt, black and red pepper to taste

Directions:

1. Preheat oven to 180 degrees.
2. Blanch the halves of the peppers in low-boiling salted water for 3 minutes.
3. Mix all other ingredients for mince.
4. Fill the halves of the peppers with stuffing.
5. Put the peppers in the form and put them in the oven.
6. Bake for 20-25 minutes.
7. Enjoy!

Nutrients per serving:

- Calories: 110.91 kcal
- Carbs: 60.5 g
- Fats: 5.3 g
- Protein: 9.40 g

Chapter 7: Side Dishes

Delicious Cauliflower Rice.

Want to turn your presentation from a side dish? I will show you how to cook cauliflower rice. It is useful, simple, very original, and very tasty. If intrigued, memorize the recipe!

Servings: 4
Prep time: 10 minutes
Cook time: 15 minutes

Ingredients:

- 1 tbsp of ghee, melted

- Juice of 2 limes
- A pinch of salt and black pepper
- 1 cup of cauliflower rice
- 1 and ½ cups of veggie stock
- 1 tbsp of cilantro, chopped

Directions:

1. Chop cauliflower in a blender.
2. Heat a pan with the ghee over medium-high heat, add the cauliflower rice, stir and cook for 5 minutes.
3. Add lime juice, salt, pepper, and stock; stir, bring to a simmer and cook for 10 minutes.
4. Add cilantro, toss, divide between plates, and serve as a side dish.

Nutrients per serving:

- Calories: 181 kcal
- Fat: 9 g
- Carbs: 2 g
- Protein: 6 g

Keto Pasta

When I want pasta, I buy zucchini and, after following the Directions, I forget about flour products for a long time.

Servings: 2

Prep time: 10 minutes

Cook time: 10 minutes

Ingredients

- 1 Zucchini
- 1 avocado
- 1 clove of garlic
- 1 sprig of basil

- 1 tbsp. of Pine nuts
- 0.5 pcs. of lemon
- Salt - to taste
- Pepper to taste
- 2 tbsp of coconut oil

Directions:

1. Prepare the sauce for zucchini. In the bowl of the blender, put coarsely chopped avocados, garlic, and basil. Add lemon juice, some pine nuts, and salt. Grind.
2. Chop Zucchini on a special grater for Korean salads. Thin straws are obtained. Chop only the upper dense part, leaving the middle that is not needed.
3. Fry the zucchini on a well-heated pan, with coconut oil, for 7 minutes.
4. Combine with sauce

Nutrients per serving:

- Calories: 443 kcal
- Fats: 38 g
- Carbs: 11.3 g
- Protein: 10 g

Spinach and Artichoke Mix

Garnish Spinach and artichoke with mozzarella are light and bright addition to meat and chicken. Also, it is very original! I recommend this simple recipe for lovers of summer vegetable dishes.

Servings: 4

Prep time: 10 minutes

Cook time: 10 minutes

Ingredients:

- 1 lb of canned artichoke hearts, drained
- A pinch of salt and black pepper

- 2 cups of baby spinach
- 2 tbsp. of parsley, chopped
- 1 cup of mozzarella, shredded
- Juice of 1 lemon
- ¾ cup of coconut milk
- 2 garlic cloves, minced
- 3 tbsp. of ghee, melted
- A pinch of red pepper flakes

Directions:

1. Heat a pan with the ghee over medium-high heat, add the garlic, stir and cook for 2 minutes.
2. Add lemon juice, coconut milk, artichokes, salt, and pepper; stir and cook for 5 minutes.
3. Add spinach, pepper flakes, and mozzarella; toss, cook for 3 minutes more. Divide between plates, sprinkle parsley on top and serve as a side dish.

Nutrients per serving:

- Calories: 277 kcal
- Fat: 11 g
- Carbs: 4 g
- Protein: 9 g

Broccoli and Spinach Puree

Spinach and broccoli puree is a very delicate and tasty dish.
I recommend that you try it!

Servings: 2
Prep time: 5 minutes
Cook time: 15 minutes

Ingredients:

- 10 oz (300 g) broccoli
- a big handful of spinach
- ¼ cup (50-70g) butter or ghee
- some pumpkin seeds, grated cheese or fried bacon for serving

- salt, pepper, herbs to taste

Directions:

1. Rub the broccoli florets. We throw them into the pan, where a small piece of butter has already melted. Fry a little, add spinach, pour a little boiling water - so that the vegetables are stewed and not fried.
2. After about 7 minutes (when broccoli becomes softer but does not turn into a clumped mass), directly in the saucepan, beat everything with a dipping blender into a homogeneous mass, and add oil. In general, the more the fat, the more delicious this mash is, so try it; you may not stop at 50 g. Add salt and pepper. Another life hack. It is tastier if you mash the salt a little bit, and when serving from above, sprinkle flakes of salt or sea salt.
3. Spread on the plates, and on top, pour the shredded cheese; for example, parmesan, roasted seeds, or crispy bacon crumb.

By the way, add a little cream in the Direction process, and you have a vegetable puree soup.

Nutrients per serving:
- Calories: 320 kcal
- Fats: 32 g
- Protein: 5 g
- Carbs: 6.5 g

Baked Broccoli Garnish

Broccoli is one of the most useful types of cabbage. But already cooked in a creamy soft sauce with cheese, it just melts in your mouth. This simple and easy side dish is fantastic for both lunch and dinner.

Servings: 4

Prep time: 10 minutes

Cook time: 15 minutes

Ingredients:

- 2 tbsp. of olive oil
- 1 broccoli head, florets separated
- 2 garlic cloves, minced
- ½ cup of mozzarella, shredded
- ¼ of cup parmesan, grated
- ½ of cup coconut cream
- 1 tbsp parsley, chopped

Directions:

1. In a heated pan, fry in oil broccoli, salt, pepper, and garlic; stir and cook for 6 minutes.

2. Add parmesan, mozzarella, and cream. Toss, introduce the pan in the oven and cook at 375 degrees F for 10 minutes.

3. Decorate with greens. Enjoy!

Nutrients per serving:

- Calories: 261 kcal
- Fat: 11 g
- Carbs: 6 g
- Protein: 8 g

Chapter 8: Snacks

Coconut Keto Candy

Do you like coconut sweets? Do you want to learn how to make such sweetness independently and at home? I offer a recipe for Directions on this excellent snack!

Serves: 10

Prep Time: 5 minutes

Total Time: 15 minutes

Ingredients:

- ⅓ cup of Coconut Butter, Softened
- ⅓ cup of Coconut Oil, Melted

- 1 oz Shredded Coconut, Unsweetened
- 1 A teaspoon of Sugar Substitute

Directions:

1. Start by mixing all of your ingredients, and make sure that the sugar substitute is well dissolved.

2. Pour into silicone molds, and then refrigerate for about an hour.

Nutrients per serving:

- Calories: 104 kcal
- Fat: 11 g
- Carbs: 0.8 g
- Protein: 0.3 g

Cheesy Cauliflower Croquettes

Cauliflower croquettes are beautiful whether hot or cold. Excellent. They go under different sauces - sharp, sweet, sour. Be sure to try the Directions of cauliflower croquettes for a snack.

Servings: 4
Prep time: 10 minutes
Cook time: 30 minutes

Ingredients:
- 2 cup. of cauliflower florets
- 2 tsp. of minced garlic
- ½ cup. of chopped onion
- ½ tsp. of salt
- ½ tsp. of pepper

- 2 tbsps. of butter
- ¾ cup. of grated cheddar cheese

Directions:

1. Place butter in a microwave-safe bowl; then melts the butter. Let it cool.
2. Place cauliflower florets in a food processor; then process until smooth and becoming crumbles.
3. Transfer the cauliflower crumbles to a bowl and then add chopped onion and cheese.
4. Season with minced garlic, salt, and pepper. Pour melted butter over the mixture.
5. Shape the cauliflower mixture into medium balls and arrange in the Air Fryer.
6. Preheat an Air Fryer to 400°F and cook the cauliflower croquettes for 14 minutes.
7. To achieve a more golden brown color, cook the cauliflower croquettes for another 2 minutes.
8. Serve and enjoy with.

Nutritional:

- Calories: 160 kcal
- Fat: 13g
- Protein: 6.8g
- Carbs: 5.1g

Kale Chips

That you have not tried! Kale leaf chips - a very refreshing homemade snack, which is not difficult to cook. If you want to please yourself and loved ones with excellent chips, prepare this recipe!

Serves: 2
Prep time: 10 minutes
Cook time: 5 minutes

Ingredients:

- 3 tsp. of olive oil
- 12 pieces of kale leaves
- Salt and pepper, as needed

Directions:

1. Preheat oven to 350°F.
2. Line a baking sheet with parchment paper.
3. Wash and thoroughly dry kale leave and place them on the baking sheet.
4. Smear kale with olive oil and sprinkle with salt and pepper.
5. Bake 10 to 15 minutes.
6. Serve.

Nutrients per serving:

- Calories: 107 kcal
- Carbs: 8.4g
- Carbs: 4.9g
- Protein: 4.11g

Keto Brownies

I suggest you learn how to make a Brownies that does not have carbohydrates. This is a very gentle, airy and easy-to-prepare Brownies.

Serves: 16

Prep time: 15 minutes

Cook time: 10 minutes

Ingredients:

- 1 cup almond butter
- 3 large eggs
- 6 oz (170g) powdered erythritol

171

- 3.5 oz (100g) unsweetened cocoa powder
- ½ tsp of baking powder
- ¼ tsp of salt

Directions:

1. Preheat oven to 325°F.
2. Using a food processor, blend the almond butter and Erythritol for about 2 minutes.
3. Add in the eggs, cocoa powder, baking powder, and a ¼ teaspoon of salt. Blend until smooth.
4. Grease the baking pan.
5. Spread the dough into forms into the baking pan, and bake for 12 minutes.
6. Let cool for 30 minutes before cutting into the desired size.
7. Enjoy!

Nutrients per serving:

- Calories: 136 kcal
- Fat: 12.54g
- Carbs: 4.21g
- Protein: 1.6g

Peanut Butter Cookie

Want to make elementary, tasty, and incredibly aromatic peanut cookies at home? Then hurry to remember this fantastic recipe for this snack and repeat it in your kitchen.

Serves: 12

Prep time: 15 minutes

Cook time: 10 minutes

Ingredients:

- 1 cup of peanut butter
- ½ cup of powdered erythritol
- 1 egg

Directions:

1. Preheat oven to 350°F.

2. In a medium bowl, combine the peanut butter, erythritol, and the egg. Mix well.

3. Form the cookie dough into 1-inch balls.

4. Place the balls on a parchment paper-lined baking sheet.

5. Press down on the dough with a fork twice, in opposite directions. Repeat with the rest of the dough.

6. Bake for about 13 minutes.

7. Let cool for 5 minutes before serving.

Nutrients per serving:

- Calories: 80 kcal
- Fat: 9.12g
- Carbs: 5.96g
- Protein: 2.91g

Minty Chocolate Fat Bombs

The recipe is for a refreshing and invigorating mint-flavored snack. Such sweets will come to your taste and will be useful.

Serves: 6

Prep Time: 10 minutes

Total Time: 20 minutes

Ingredients:

- ½ Cup of Coconut Oil, Melted
- 2 tbsp. of Cocoa Powder
- 1 tbsp of Granulated Stevia (or sweetener of choice)

- ½ tsp of Peppermint Essence

Directions:

1. Start by melting your coconut oil, and adding your peppermint essence and sweetener.
2. Add cocoa powder to half of the mixture and mix well in another bowl.
3. Pour the chocolate mixture into the silicone molds, and then place them in the fridge. Refrigerate for 5-10 minutes.
4. Make the mint layer by pouring the mint mixture into the silicone molds. Refrigerate and let it harden.

Nutrients per serving:

- Calories: 161 kcal
- Total Fat: 18.5 g
- Carbs: 0.45 g
- Protein: 0.4 g

Chapter 9: Ketogenic Sauces

Avocado & Yogurt Sauce with Salad Cilantro

This sauce is excellent for salad dressing. You can also try it with meat. The main ingredients of the sauce are perfectly combined. Lime gives a few citrus notes, and garlic and pepper make it spicier.
It is prepared very quickly because all the ingredients are mixed in a grinder.

Prepare time: 15 minutes

Ingredients:

- 1 avocado
- 2 tbsp. of cilantro
- 1 garlic clove
- 1 tbsp of lime juice
- 1/4 tsp of black pepper
- 1/4 of teaspoon salt
- 3 tbsp. of olive oil
- ½ cup Greek yogurt

Directions:

1. Put the ingredients in the chopper bowl and chop to the desired consistency.

   You can fill them with salad.

Nutrients per serving:

- Carbs: 381 g
- Fat: 11.72 g
- Protein: 2.1 g
- Calories: 123 kcal

Keto Parmesan Pesto

We strongly recommend that you learn how to make a homemade "Pesto" sauce - an incredibly creamy egg sauce with a bright, refreshing taste that is suitable for chips, snacks, and salads!

Serves: 6 (about two tbsp.)
Prep Time: 5 minutes
Total Time: 5 minutes

Ingredients:

- 1 Cup Full of Fat Cream Cheese
- 2 tbsp. of Basil Pesto
- ½ cup of Parmesan Cheese, Grated
- 8 Olives, Sliced
- Salt and Pepper to Taste

Directions:

1. Mix all of your ingredients in a mixing bowl.
2. Refrigerate for at least 20 minutes before serving.

Nutrients per serving:

- Calories: 161 kcal
- Fat: 14.33 g
- Carbs: 3.23 g
- Protein: 5.42 g

Salsa Sauce

The high-quality sauce can significantly improve the taste of the dish, as well as give unusual flavors. This is especially true for spicy additives. They are often used in recipes of Mexican cuisine.

Prepare time: 5 minutes

Ingredients:

- 3 tbsp of cider vinegar
- 4 tbsp of olive oil
- 2 tbsp of sour cream

- 2 tbsp of mayo
- 1 tsp of chili powder
- 1 garlic clove
- ½ cup of salsa sauce

Directions:

1. Whisk all ingredients in the bowl until smooth. Or you can shake them all together in a tight-fitting jar.
2. Season it to your taste. You can dilute it with water if you want a thinner sauce.

Nutrients per serving:

- Carbs: 2 g
- Fat: 21 g
- Protein: 1 g
- Calories: 200 kcal

Blue Cheese Sauce

From a few simple ingredients in just 5 minutes, you can make a fresh sauce. It will complement the pizza, sandwiches, vegetables, as well as zucchini pasta, and favorite snacks. Great recipe!

Prepare time: 5 minutes

Ingredients:
- ¾ cup of Greek yogurt
- 5 oz of bleu cheese
- ½ cup of mayo
- Heavy whipping cream

- 2 tbsp of fresh parsley
- Salt and pepper

Directions:

1. Break the cheese into chunks in a small bowl, and then add yogurt and mayo before mixing well.
2. Let it sit for a few minutes.
3. Dilute in water or heavy cream for your desired consistency and season with greens, salt, and pepper.

Nutrients per serving:

- Carbs: 3 g
- Fat: 36 g
- Protein: 9 g
- Calories: 375 kcal

Thai Peanut Sauce

I recommend peanut butter sauce to lovers of all original and new recipes. With it, any meat dish or a simple chicken will play with new colors! Watch and write!

Prepare time: 8 minutes

Ingredients:

- ½ oz of ginger root
- ½ tbsp. of garlic
- ¼ tsp. of molasses
- ½ cup of peanut butter
- 1 tbsp. of Stevia

- 1 tbsp. of sesame oil
- 3 tbsp of chicken broth
- 3 tbsp of soy sauce
- 3 tbsp of hot sauce
- 2 tbsp of lime juice

Directions:

1. Mix all ingredients smoothly.
2. Place it in a jar and cover it.
3. Leave it for at least a night before using, and store it in the refrigerator.

Nutrients per serving:

- Calories: 158 kcal
- Fat: 13 g
- Protein: 6 g
- Carbs: 3 g

Chapter 10: Desserts

Ice Cream with Avocado

Do you like ice cream? Today, I will tell you how to make a tasty and straightforward avocado ice cream at home! Everything is straightforward and fast; even no special equipment is needed!

Servings: 6

Prep time: 10 minutes

Cook time: 30 minutes

Ingredients:

- 1 peeled and pitted the avocado
- 1½ tsp. of vanilla paste
- 1 cup. of coconut milk
- 2 tbsp of almond butter
- Drops of stevia
- ¼ tsp. of Ceylon cinnamon

Directions:

1. Combine all ingredients in a food blender.
2. Blend until smooth.
3. Transfer the mixture into Popsicle molds and insert popsicle sticks.
4. Freeze for 4 hours or until firm.
5. Serve.

Nutrients per serving:

- Calories: 41 kcal
- Fats: 10 g
- Net Carbs 0.1 g
- Protein 0 g

Delicious Brownies

Diet is not a reason to deny yourself of the pleasure of indulging in sweets. You only need to choose the right sweets. For example, cook a low-carb brownie.

Servings: 4

Prep time: 10 minutes

Cook time: 25 minutes

Ingredients:

- 5 oz of chocolate 86% (sugarless); melted
- 4 tbsp. of ghee, melted
- 3 eggs

- ½ cup of Swerve
- ¼ cup of mascarpone cheese
- ¼ cup of cocoa powder

Directions:

1. Take a big bowl; combine the melted chocolate with the ghee, eggs, swerve, cheese and cocoa. Whisk well, pour into a cake pan, introduce in the oven and cook at 375 degrees F for 25 minutes.
2. Cut into medium brownies and serve.

Nutrients per serving:

- Calories 120 kcal
- Fat: 8 g
- Carbs: 3 g
- Protein: 3 g

Chocolate Keto Cake with Blueberry

This is an ordinary cake that is very tasty and will appeal even to those who do not eat according to the keto-diet. My son, who is skeptical of any keto desserts, tried it and approved it. So go for it!
In it, of course, there is cottage cheese. But use the fattest curd. All together - this is a real fat bomb! It's nutrient profile is very keto.

Servings: 8

Prepare time: 10 minutes

Cook time: 40 minutes

Ingredients:

- 2 eggs, stripped into whites and yolks
- 1 tbsp (25 g) of cocoa powder
- 1/3 cup (50 g) of almond flour
- 2 tbsp (20 g) pf flax flour
- 1 tsp. of sweetener (or to taste)
- 2/3 cup (150 g) of sour cream
- 2.5 tbsp (50 g) of vegetable oil
- 2 tsp. of baking powder
- Vanilla or vanilla extract to taste

Directions:

1. Turn on the oven to 350 F degrees.
2. Beat the squirrel to stable foam.
3. Beat yolks with sweetener.
4. Add sour cream and vegetable oil and mix.
5. Add all the dry ingredients and mix again, you can use a mixer.
6. Add proteins in two steps and mix them gently into the dough.
7. Use the form 16 cm in diameter.
8. Put in the oven for 25 minutes.
9. Cut the cake into two. You can soak them with a mixture of 1 tbsp. of water and 1 tsp. of Liquor.

10. For the cream, beat all ingredients with a mixer.

11. Spread the cake and put the cake in the fridge to soak over the night.

Nutrients per serving (105g):

- Calories: 295,50 kcal
- Fat: 27.65 g
- Carbs: 7, 94 g
- Protein: 7.25 g

Chocolate Mousse

Chocolate mousse is an exquisite delicacy that can be served at a party as a dessert; make an airy layer of chocolate cake. Help yourself!

Servings: 4

Prepare time: 5 minutes

Cook time: 5 minutes

Ingredients:

- 1 tbsp. of cocoa powder
- 2 oz of cream cheese
- 2 oz of butter

- 3 oz. of heavy whipping cream
- Stevia to taste

Directions:

1. Melt the butter a bit and mix with the sweetener. Stir until blended.
2. Add the cream cheese and cocoa powder and blend until smooth.
3. Carefully whip heavy cream and gradually add to the mixture.
4. Refrigerate it for 30 mins.

Nutrients per serving:

- Calories: 227 kcal
- Fat: 24 g
- Carbs: 3 g
- Protein: 4 g

Coconut Raspberry Cake

Sweet tooth, attention! Today I want to share with you just a fantastic recipe for coconut cake; very gentle and melting in your mouth! Be sure to prepare it for the next holiday!

Servings: 6

Preparation time: 1 hour and 10 minutes

Cook time: 10 Minutes.

Ingredients:

For the biscuit:

- 2 cups almond flour
- 1 egg

- 1 tbsp of ghee, melted
- ½ tsp of baking soda
- For the coconut layer:
- 1 cup of coconut milk
- ¼ cup of coconut oil, melted
- 3 cups coconut, shredded
- 1/3 cup of stevia
- 1 tsp (5 g) of food gelatin

For the raspberry layer:
- 1 cup of raspberries
- 1 tsp of stevia
- 3 tbsp. of chia seeds
- 1 tsp (5 g) of food gelatin

Directions:

1. In a bowl, combine the almond flour with the eggs, ghee and baking soda; stir well. Press on the bottom of the springform pan, and introduce in the oven at 350 degrees F for 15 minutes. Leave aside to cool down.

2. Meanwhile, in a pan, combine the raspberries with 1-teaspoon stevia, chia seeds, and gelatin; stir, and cook for 5 minutes. Take off the heat, cool down and spread over the biscuit layer.

3. In another small pan, combine the coconut milk with the coconut, oil, gelatin, 1/3 cup stevia; stir for 1-2 minutes. Take off the heat, cool down and spread over the coconut milk.

4. Cool the cake in the fridge for 1 hour, slice and serve.

Nutrients per serving:

- Calories: 241 kcal
- Fat: 12 g
- Fiber: 4 g
- Carbs: 5 g
- Protein: 5 g

21-DAY MEAL PLAN

This 21-day meal plan will help you easily organize your meal! In this section, you will find weekly meal plans with breakfast, lunch, snacks, and dinner.

How to use the 21-day meal plan

• Check your weekly meal plan and recipes in advance and make the necessary purchases.

• Set up a meal plan: you do not need to strictly adhere to this plan; boldly replace them with other recipes or ingredients that are keto-friendly.

• For lunches and snacks on weekdays, you can prepare them in advance and store them in containers so that you can take them when you go to work. You can even pack the leftover dinner for the next day.

Week One Meal Plan

DAY 1 (MONDAY)

- Breakfast: Bulletproof coffee
- Lunch: Zucchini Noodle Shrimp
- Dinner: Stuffed Chicken Peppers

Day 2 (Tuesday)

- Breakfast: Perfect Keto Pancakes
- Lunch: Keto Lasagna
- Dinner: Fried minced dinner with zucchini and pepper

Day 3 (Wednesday)

- Breakfast: Egg muffins with broccoli for breakfast
- Lunch: Citrus Tilapia
- Dinner: Crispy Zucchini Pancakes

Day 4 (Thursday)

- Breakfast: Seafood Omelet
- Lunch: Keto Meatloaf and Delicious cauliflower rice
- Dinner: Creamy Broccoli and Leek Soup

Day 5 (Friday)

- Breakfast: Salad Sandwich
- Lunch: Baked cauliflower with cheese
- Dinner: Burrito in the salad leaves with turkey

Day 6 (Saturday)

- Breakfast: Vegetable casserole
- Lunch: Goat Cheese Omelet and Avocado & Yogurt Sauce with Salad Cilantro
- Dinner: Keto Sushi

Day 7 (Sunday)

- Breakfast: Low-Carb Sour berry cake
- Lunch: Keto "Fried" Chicken and Baked Broccoli Garnish
- Dinner: Baked zucchini with cheese

Week Two Meal Plan

DAY 8 (MONDAY)

- Breakfast: Ground Beef and Creamy Cauliflower Made in a Skillet
- Lunch: Baked cauliflower with cheese
- Dinner: Rissole in bacon

Day 9 (Tuesday)

- Breakfast: Coconut breakfast cereal
- Lunch: Chicken with vegetables and Salsa Sauce
- Dinner: Cheesy Broccoli Soup

Day 10 (Wednesday)

- Breakfast: Stuffed avocado
- Lunch: Chicken with mushrooms in a creamy sauce
- Dinner: Fried minced dinner with zucchini and pepper

Day 11 (Thursday)

- Breakfast: Bulletproof coffee
- Lunch: Baked Salmon with Lemon and Spinach and Artichoke Mix
- Dinner: Crispy Zucchini Pancakes

Day 12 (Friday)

- Breakfast: Boiled Eggs with Mayo
- Lunch: Soup Egg and Lemon with Chicken
- Dinner: Baked zucchini with cheese

Day 13 (Saturday)

- Breakfast: Awesome Breakfast Salad
- Lunch: Zucchini Noodle Shrimp and Keto Parmesan Pesto
- Dinner: Stuffed Chicken Peppers

Day 14 (Sunday)

- Breakfast: Eggs in nests
- Lunch: Keto Lasagna
- Dinner: Burrito in the salad leaves with turkey

Week Three Meal Plan

DAY 15 (MONDAY)

- Breakfast: Cauliflower Fritters
- Lunch: Citrus Tilapia and Broccoli and Spinach Puree
- Dinner: Chicken with Lemon and Garlic

Day 16 (Tuesday)

- Breakfast: Seafood Omelet
- Lunch: Keto Meatloaf and Salsa Sauce
- Dinner: Cheesy Broccoli Soup

Day 17 (Wednesday)

- Breakfast: Vegetable casserole
- Lunch: Goat Cheese Omelet
- Dinner: Keto Sushi

Day 18 (Thursday)

- Breakfast: Bulletproof coffee
- Lunch: Baked cauliflower with cheese
- Dinner: Creamy Broccoli and Leek Soup

Day 19 (Friday)

- Breakfast: Perfect Keto Pancakes

- Lunch: Keto "Fried" Chicken and Blue Cheese Sauce
- Dinner: Burrito in the salad leaves with turkey

Day 20 (Saturday)

- Breakfast: Egg muffins with broccoli for breakfast
- Lunch: Chicken with mushrooms in a creamy sauce
- Dinner: Stuffed Chicken Peppers

Day 21 (Sunday)

- Breakfast: Bulletproof coffee
- Lunch: Baked cauliflower with cheese
- Dinner: Crispy Zucchini Pancakes

Conclusion

What we will say is that keto is not a diet; it is a way of life, it is a lifestyle, and it is health. It is an opportunity not only to lose weight but also to cure the body and prevent various diseases.

Thanks again for downloading this book!

We hope that this book has been able to help you understand the ketogenic diet and learn how to prepare various ketogenic recipes.

Kitchen Conversions

Weight conversions

METRIC	CUPS	OUNCES
15 g	1 tablespoon	1/2 ounce
30 g	1/8 cup	1 ounce
60 g	1/4 cup	2 ounces
115 g	1/2 cup	4 ounces
170 g	3/4 cup	6 ounces
225 g	1 cup	8 ounces
450 g	2 cups	16 ounces

Oven temperatures

CELSIUS	FAHRENHEIT
95°C	200°F
130°C	250°F
150°C	300°F
160°C	325°F
175°C	350°F
190°C	375°F
200°C	400°F
230°C	450°F

Length

METRIC	IMPERIAL
3 mm	1/8 inch
6 mm	1/4 inch
2.5 cm	1 inch
3 cm	1 1/4 inch
5 cm	2 inches
10 cm	4 inches
15 cm	6 inches
20 cm	8 inches
22.5 cm	9 inches
25 cm	10 inches
28 cm	11 inches

Volume conversions

METRIC	CUPS	OUNCES
15 ml	1 tablespoon	1/2 fl. oz
30 ml	2 tablespoons	1 fl. oz
60 ml	1/4 cup	2 fl. oz
125 ml	1/2 cup	4 fl. oz
180 ml	3/4 cup	6 fl. oz
250 ml	1 cup	8 fl. oz
500 ml	2 cups	16 fl. oz
1000 ml	4 cups	1 quart

Keto friendly sweeteners

Stevia	Xylitol
Sucralose	Monk fruit sweetener
Erythritol	Yacon syrup

Product	Calories	Fat	Carbohydrates	Protein
Celery	13	0.1	3	0.6
Zucchini	14.4	0	3.5	0.6
Avocado	47	4.4	0.6	0.6
Cauliflower	7	0.1	0.5	0.5
Bell pepper	6	0	0.8	0.2
Tomato	18.9	0.3	4.2	0.8
Spinach	20.7	0.2	3.4	2.7
Mushrooms	21.1	0.4	4	1.7

Onion	30.4	0.1	6.9	0.9
Beef	213	17	0	
Chicken	284	6.2	0	53.4
Salmon	412	27	0	40
Cod	189	1.5	0	41
Garlic	1	0	0.2	0
Rutabagas	19	0.1	0.5	3.2
Kohlrabi	20	0.1	1.3	2
Ghee	34	3.8	0	0
Salt, Sea salt	0	0	0	0
Pepper	0	0	0	0.1
Egg yolk	55	4.5	2.7	0.6
Parsley	1	0	0.1	0.1
Olive Oil	119	13.5	0	0
Rosemary	0	0	0	0

Mustard	0	0.3	0.3	0.1
Red wine	48	0	0	1.5
Bacon	44	3.5	0	2.9
Egg	72	4.8	0.4	6.3
Hot dog	92	8.5	0.5	3.1
Tuna	52	1.8	0	8.5
Shrimp	28	0.1	0	6.8
Scallops	31	0.2	1.5	5.8
Pork Chop	65	4.1	0	6.7
Old Wisconsin Beef Summer Sausage	200	18	0	9
Hickory Farms Beef Summer Sausage	180	15	1	10
Armour Vienna Sausage	117	9	1	6
Wisconsin's Best – Pit-Smoked Summer Sausage	66	5	1	3

Butter	102	12	0	0
Olive oil	119	13.5	0	0
Coconut oil	117	13.6	0	0
Cheddar Cheese	114	9.4	0.4	7.1
Cream Cheese	97	9.7	1.1	1.7
Feta Cheese	75	6	1.2	4
Heavy Cream	103	11	0.8	0.6
Sour cream	55	5.6	0.8	0.6
Parmesan Cheese	111	7.3	0.9	10.0
Mozzarella Cheese	85	6.3	0.6	6.3
Cashews	160	1	7	5
Sesame Seeds	160	14	4	5
Flax seeds	131	10	0	7
Walnuts	185	18	2	4

Made in the USA
Las Vegas, NV
24 May 2023

72466043R10118